The *Keeper of*

LIME
ROCK

RUNNING PRESS
PHILADELPHIA · LONDON

Praise for *The Keeper of Lime Rock*

✦✦✦

"[A] spellbinding story of the era and the woman, who was a quiet feminist before the word was coined."
—*The Oakland Press*

"Numerous photographs, notes and a bibliography do justice to this remarkable . . . heroine."
—*Cape Cod Times*

"Lenore Skomal . . . treats her solid historical homework briskly and lightly . . . Fascinating."
—*The Providence Journal*

"Oddly compelling book is of a tiny tigress . . . all of 103 pounds, bound to a lonely speck of rock."
—*Philadelphia Inquirer*

"Meticulously researched . . . recounts the story of Ida Lewis and other courageous women who tended the precious fresnel lenses . . . ."
—*Standard-Times*, New Bedford

"Lenore Skomal is to be lauded for saving this bit of history."
—*Martha's Vineyard* magazine

"*The Keeper of Lime Rock* presents a glimpse into another age and the challenges lighthouse keepers faced every day."
—Lou Belcher, *The Virginian-Pilot*

"A compelling portrait."
—*School Library Journal*

The Keeper of Lime Rock

The Remarkable True Story of Ida Lewis,
America's Most Celebrated Lighthouse Keeper

by Lenore Skomal

RUNNING PRESS
PHILADELPHIA · LONDON

9 8 7 6 5 4 3 2 1
Digit on the right indicates the number of this printing
First paperback edition published in 2003

Library of Congress Cataloging-in-Publication Number 2001094679

ISBN 0-7624-1538-X

Cover illustration: Copyright © 2001 VCG/Getty Images
Cover design by Whitney Cookman
Design by Serrin Bodmer
Edited by Jennifer Worick
Typography: AGaramond, Goudy,
Cezanne, Vendome ICG, and Webdings
Map of Newport Harbor courtesy of the Newport Historical Society

This book may be ordered by mail from the publisher.
Please include $2.50 for postage and handling.
But try your bookstore first!

Running Press Book Publishers
125 South Twenty-second Street
Philadelphia, Pennsylvania 19103-4399

Visit us on the web!
www.runningpress.com

This book is dedicated to my parents—the late and loving Irene Homoky Skomal, keeper of our family light, and Bernard J. Skomal, who paid for the oil. Keep the light on for us, Mom, wherever you are.

Contents

Acknowledgments

Separating fact from fiction has been the yeoman's task in writing this book. There are virtually no primary sources that I could find in Ida's own hand about her life as the keeper of Lime Rock. Ida apparently kept no diaries. There are no personal letters or correspondences, as far as I could find, that have survived in her wake or are readily traceable. It is questionable whether she wrote much during her lifetime. It has been posed that she may have been functionally illiterate. I doubt this is true, as she was an avid reader of the Bible and had to fill out rudimentary logs and reports routinely in her capacity as keeper. Perhaps she was simply not comfortable with the pen.

Secondary and tertiary resources are not the most reliable. In many instances throughout this book, dates have been verified to the best of my ability, but sometimes conflict with newspaper accounts, journal articles, and published and unpublished accounts. Ida Lewis did authorize Colonel George Brewerton, a Newport journalist at the time, to write about the first five rescues in which she was involved. The sixty-six-page booklet survives, but provides little in exacting detail and is really a recounting of Ida's *memories* of her own rescues, embellished considerably by the author.

✦ ✦ ✦

Many people were instrumental in what can only be called the "detective work" behind this book, which has been truly a labor of love.

This book would have few photos without the generosity of Mark Kellner, manager of the Ida Lewis Yacht Club in Newport, who graciously gave of his time on several occasions, and readily contributed the club's personal photo collection of the heroine. Not only has this added to the richness and color of this text, it has given the reader the rare opportunity to view photos that have never before been published. The club's interest in preserving the legacy of Ida Lewis was the fundamental mission of its founding and the club and its personnel should be applauded for the job they are doing.

James Nolda, Senior Chief Petty Officer of the U.S. Coast Guard's cutter *IDA LEWIS,* was of great help in securing photos and information about his ship. In addition, he connected me with the right sources to help with the historical details about the background of the Lighthouse Service. He even offered me the chance to come aboard *IDA LEWIS* and watch the heroine's legacy in action. The Coast Guard also named a training center in Cape May, New Jersey, after Ida in October 2001.

A note of gratitude to the Newport Historical Society where I retrieved much of my initial information about Ida Lewis. By and far, the librarians at New York Public Library in Manhattan deserve special commendation for their eagerness to help and willingness to educate me in the process of research in their vast collection of antiquated materials. The NYPL is truly a treasure trove of resources. A special thanks to the Bridgeport Public Library, especially librarian Roseanne Mansfield, who worked with me, in vain, to try to find any shred of evidence that would shed some light on the mystery that is William H. Wilson, husband of Ida Lewis.

Especially crucial was the verification of the medals Ida received. The more accounts I read, the more confusing the list of medals and honors became. Inaccuracy creates confusion and I would be unerringly remiss not to express my heartfelt thanks to the Order and Medals Society of America (OMSA), based in Illinois. Since many of the associations that recognized Ida are no longer in existence, enthusiasts and buffs like members of OMSA have provided a true service in lending credibility to the text herein. The members were eager to share their knowledge and went to considerable lengths to help me. OMSA president Douglas Boyce was instrumental in explaining the differences in medals and in helping me verify several of the medals Ida Lewis was awarded in her lifetime. Jack Boddington, a prolific Canadian writer in his own right, spent hours of his time helping me find several other awards and medals, photocopying text, and mailing all of it to me, along with books from his own collection. Ron Fischer lent his expertise in giving me background on the Cross of Honor. The Yachting Museum at Fort Adams houses the actual boat *Rescue.* Several small medals are kept at the Newport Historical Society, along with a pocket Bible belonging to Ida Lewis and the silver filigree teapot given to her by the soldiers at Fort Adams. The Historical Society's museum displays the actual lantern that Ida tended, along with a brief history of the lighthouse keeper. Early correspondences housed at the Ida Lewis Yacht Club indicates that the original founding fathers of the Club were in possession of Ida's medals at one point, when they purchased the lighthouse and island from the government. They apparently handed the items, including the gold U.S. Lifesaving Medal, over to the Newport Historical Society in the "fifties or sixties," according to yacht club member Arthur Dyer. But the society does not have them in its possession.

The staffs at the several branches of the National Archives (NARA) helped with background information about weather, lighthouse logs, and photographs, in Maryland, Washington, D.C., and Waltham, Massachusetts.

While most photographs were lent by the Ida Lewis Yacht Club, others were acquired through the United States Coast Guard Historian's office, the National Archives, the Library of Congress, the Newport Historical Society, and the hard work of my father, Bernard J. Skomal, a fine photographer in his own right.

Lastly, and certainly not least, a heartfelt thanks for all those close to me who have wished me well on this endeavor and rejoiced along with me in its completion. I am fortunate that they are many. Specifically, I would be remiss not to single out Running Press Associate Publisher and friend Carlo DeVito, who took the chance on me; my excellent, funny editor Jennifer Worick, who tried not to step on my ego; my sweet son Nate, on whom the sun will always rise and set; my dear family, especially my wonderful father and wayward travel companion, Bernie J., and my little sister, stalwart baby-sitter Aunt Maggie; and cub reporter and researcher Jimmy Dick, who believed in me and this project from the very beginning.

On a final note, for all those who need to write, I believe the world needs to read. Don't stop. Don't forget.

Chapter 1
Propelled to Notoriety

When she performed this duty she had no thought of its being recognized. In fact, I believe if she thought what men would say about it, probably the act never would have been done at all.
—Colonel Thomas Wentworth Higginson,
speaking of Ida's rescue

The wintry gale was coming in fast and furious, whipping the water around Lime Rock Lighthouse into a roiling frenzy, and sending icy blasts of wind against the house, clattering the windows of the kitchen.

It was March 29, 1869.

Early spring meant an influx of storms into the harbor, which chopped up the still-icy seas, and brought spring thaw in with a vengeance. It was 5:00 P.M., and Ida had taken a few minutes to sit in her favorite chair near the hearth before preparing dinner. She had been sick with a terrible cold, and was trying to collect herself for the night's work ahead. As she soaked her feet in warm water, she heard her mother rustling in the other part of the house. Ida Zoradia—known simply as Zoradia so as not to be confused with her namesake daughter—had gone to her room to lie down. She was weary from taking care of her now almost completely disabled husband and her other daughter, Hattie, whose lungs were never strong and who often suffered through the long winter with an infectious cough.

But Zoradia couldn't rest, being nagged by the sense that something was amiss. Like her daughter Ida, she was uncomfortable being idle, so she decided to check the oil supply for the nightly lamp. She rose from her bed, and made her way to the passageway that led to the lantern room. The view atop the cramped lantern room was a familiar one, so the smallest change on the horizon was immediately noticeable and called for closer attention. She checked the oil supply, and took one more sweep of the harbor and open sea with her gaze.

She froze and peered through the now-falling snow closely. She spied an overturned boat, with what appeared to be two men clinging to its hull and yelling for help. In the fury of the sea, the capsized boat was also drifting toward Goat Island, moving out of the harbor into the open channel toward the ocean. And it was moving swiftly in the billowing waves of the stormy sea.

Filled with terror, she called to her daughter. "Ida, O my God! Ida, run quick! A boat has capsized and men are drowning. Run quick, Ida!" Ida only caught the "drowning men" reference and was on her feet. Her invalid father frantically tried to dissuade her from racing out the door. He shouted after her that it wasn't her duty to fish the "addled of brain" out of the water. Any sailor who ventures out in a storm knows the danger involved and should expect the worst, he added.

Ida barely heard him. She was already to the boat. She neglected to take the time to put on her button-up boots, hat, overcoat, or even a shawl. She merely grabbed a towel, which she twisted about her neck as she raced toward the boat. Time was of the essence. A matter of seconds could mean the difference between life and death. As she slipped her way across the bone-biting limestones, her feet were cut by the edges of sharp rocks. She yelled back to her younger brother Hosea, known as "Hosey," to come help her. He followed suit, joining her in the boat.

The hard wind and driving rain railed against her back as she pulled the oars with a strength equal to a hearty male. At times, it felt as if she alone was pulling the skiff, setting the rhythm of the oars against the overwhelming power of the sea, all the while barking orders at Hosey. Her strength, both physical and emotional, superseded his, powered by her overwhelming sense of duty and single-minded courage. The sea rose high around them, the icy water pouring over the boat's sides. The snow was wet and driving, hitting them with the fury of tiny spikes. Despite their hard rowing, the boat moved maddeningly slowly toward the deepest end of the harbor near Goat Island.

She could hear the desperate cries of the drowning men, a haunting distant din that made her feel frantic. Desperation was never an emotion that Ida allowed during her rescues. This time was no exception; she caught herself. She had to keep rowing, to keep focused on getting to those men, and block everything else out.

The wind seemed to play with her hearing. She thought she heard a female's voice calling. She did. Casting a glance back toward the shore of Lime Rock, Ida's mother stood on the precarious edge of the rock's furthermost point, wildly waving her arms. She was trying to signal to the panicked drowning men, by sending gestures and words of encourage-

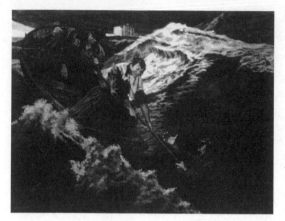

A painting of Ida rescuing two men, commissioned by the U.S. Coast Guard.

ment over the raging gale. They would later tell Zoradia that it was her cries that drew their attention to the lifeboat. They had been certain that they were facing death, and were close to giving up.

Ida set the oars further into the oncoming seas, summoning up a renewed reservoir of strength. She stroked the waves contemptuously, conscious that every effort was a battle against time, tide, and an angry storm.

Despite all odds, the small skiff, pitching wildly and taking on water rapidly, reached the drifting, overturned wreck. Ida was exhausted from the brute force that she had to expend just to get the skiff into the middle of the harbor. Her arms were cramping and her extremities were numb. With the necessary help and strength of Hosey, the two managed to pull the screaming soldiers into the boat. The two soldiers, Sergeant James Adams and Private John McLoughlin, were from nearby Fort Adams. They were in bad shape. Making it back to shore took double the effort and twice as long. Ida's only concern—over and above her own physical fatigue, pain, and early stages of hypothermia—was getting them back to shore before one of them died from exposure.

Sergeant Adams, once on the lighthouse island, was barely able to "totter up to their house." McLoughlin was unconscious. He had to be removed from the boat and hoisted into the house by the combined efforts of Ida and Hosey. It took a long time to revive him and he almost didn't make it. The pair stayed at the house through the night, where they were nursed back to reasonable health.

There had been a third person in the boat: a younger boy, whom the two reckless soldiers had hired to steer the boat. The fourteen-year-old lad was confident that he could skipper the small boat from the shore to the adjacent peninsula where Fort Adams was situated. With the onset of the storm, he clearly was not qualified to captain the boat, which took on water and eventually capsized. Waves crashed continually over the boat, and since he was swallowing gulps of icy saltwater, the boy was unable to hang onto the slippery hull of the overturned skiff. He slipped into the bitter depths of the harbor. "The boy, if the fault were his, has already paid the penalty with his young life, having gone down to rise no more, till the slow processes of decomposition, shall cause the mutilated corpse to loose its death grip from the treacherous weeds, and drift on shore..."*

Ida's other brother Rudolph would later recount the night's events. "Sergeant Adams, one of the rescued party, stated when he recovered, 'When I saw the boat approaching and a woman rowing, I thought, *She's only a woman and she will never reach us.* But I soon changed my mind.'"

About the event, Ida would later recall: "I remember one twilight in 1869. I heard the cries of two men during an awful storm. I put for them in my boat. I could see them clinging to their frail boat. I managed to pull them in, but they were nearly gone when I reached the shore."

It took hours in front of the embers of the hearth to warm herself, calm her chattering teeth, and thaw her itching, frost-

---

* From *Ida Lewis, the Heroine of Lime Rock,* Colonel George A. Brewerton, 1869.

bitten feet. She was dreadfully ill with a bad cold, and it would take her some time to fully recuperate. But she still rowed the two men to shore upon their recovery.

The last thing going through Ida's mind was fame. Unlike her previous rescues, however, this one would change her life forever.

✦ ✦ ✦

Until that time, she was simply Ida Lewis, daughter of Hosea, the stricken lighthouse keeper, and Ida Zoradia. Simply Ida Lewis, one of the four surviving children of the six born in a marriage. She was just part of this family that lived on Lime Rock and tended to its lighthouse. She was the lighthouse keeper's daughter, like so many other lighthouse keeper's daughters up and down the Atlantic seaboard, who shared in the responsibilities of keeping the light. In her case, Ida helped to tend to the rather mundane existence on the island, which was situated in the inner part of Narragansett Harbor, some 220 yards from the nearest point on shore.

Born and bred in Newport, Ida had no knowledge of how unique she was. While other lighthouse keeper's daughters may have been like her, she was definitely not like them.

Ida saved people from drowning. She did it often, and with great success.

Until March 29, 1869, no one but her family and those she pulled out of Newport Harbor knew of her extraordinary feats. A few would make the local newspaper in the form of one- or two-line briefs, but none made the headlines. Until now.

How did it happen that, overnight, she would become the toast of Newport and even the nation?

When Ida risked her life in what is considered one of her most dangerous rescues, it was indeed covered in the local paper. This was likely because it drew a response from Fort

Adams and was brought to the attention of the customs collector, who was the conduit for much information that made its way off the island of Aquidneck, where Newport is located. The account was so sensational that it was telegrammed to newspapers in New York. Upon reading the account, a reporter made the journey from the *New York Tribune* to Newport to meet this extraordinary woman. That article detailed the perilous event—considered her fifth documented rescue. It also tied her name to Grace Darling for the first time in print. Grace Darling had become somewhat of a folk hero around the world following a daring rescue in the late 1830s off the English coast.

The story goes that twenty-three-year-old Grace Darling, also a daughter of a lighthouse keeper at Longstone lighthouse, risked her life in a raging September storm, when she launched a small boat with the very reluctant aid of her father to save nine lives from a wrecked steamship. She became an instant hero, and her name became a synonym for an unselfish, heroic woman. By the time Ida was twenty-three, she had already surpassed Grace Darling's single heroic act four times over.

Grace was truly the "darling" of early Victorian society. She was born on November 24, 1815, in the English village of Bamburgh. When Grace was eleven, her father was appointed the keeper of the Longstone Light.

She was only twenty-two years old when, on duty at 4:45 in the morning of September 7, 1838, she became aware of a shipwreck during a fierce storm. The paddle steamer *S.S. Forfarshire,* carrying sixty-three people, had passed the lighthouse when its engines failed. Drifting further north, the captain hoisted sail and headed south for shelter. Eventually the ship struck a huge rocky shoal and broke in half: the stern broke away and the fore part of the ship wedged itself on a rock.

Grace reported the wreck to her father, but had to wait

until the storm had abated somewhat. Watching until dawn from her bedroom window in the lighthouse, they saw survivors clinging to the wreckage on top of the rock. Grace and her father attempted a rescue of the survivors in a coble, a twenty-foot rowboat that normally took three men to operate in bad weather. Shortly after 7:00 that morning, William and Grace set off, but could not get directly to the wreck. Rather, the pair had to go a mile out of the way to skirt the storm behind rocks and islands.

William got himself onto the rock, leaving Grace alone in the boat. They managed to pick up four men and a woman, and only got back to the lighthouse with the extra help of the rescued men. William Darling and two of the rescued men then returned to pick up the last four survivors while Grace stayed at the lighthouse with her mother to look after the first round of survivors. The nine were taken care of and fed at the lighthouse until the storm abated two days later, at which time they were taken to the mainland. All the other passengers and crew drowned.

When news of the rescue broke, Grace became a national heroine overnight, much to her consternation. She was awarded the gold medal of the Humane Society and received fifty pounds from the Treasury. An additional 750 pounds were raised by public subscription for her. Her portrait was painted many times over. Wordsworth and other poets penned poems about her courageous feat. She had numerous requests for locks of her hair (to the point where she joked she was going bald). She even had proposals of marriage. In the best tradition of the Victorian theater, the Adelphi Theatre in London proposed (unsuccessfully) to have Grace appear nightly to depict her story on stage.

She tried to hide in the distant northeast that was her home, denying that she had done anything particularly courageous. Such peace did not last long as Grace died of consumption on October 20, 1842, at the young age of twenty-six. That same year, the woman who would become her namesake was born a continent away.

Grace Darling was buried in Bamburgh churchyard in the family tomb, but such was her fame that sailors wanted to be reminded of her as they sailed pasted the Farnes. Consequently, a memorial was erected in the churchyard in sight of the sea. Grace was a reluctant heroine, much as Ida would prove to be.

On the heels of the Tribune article of April 15, 1869, *Harper's Weekly* and *Frank Leslie's Illustrated Newspaper* followed suit, sending artists along with their reporters to sketch Ida for engravings for their upcoming editions. The combined circulation of these publications ensured that tens of thousands of people would read about Ida Lewis in just a few days.

She was on her way to becoming a household name.

✦ ✦ ✦

Ida's star reached its zenith a few months later in the middle of summer. It was Saturday, July 4, 1869. The skies over Newport were cloudy and the air was warm and sticky. Thanks to the breezes from the harbor, what would have been a stifling morning in any landlocked place proved nicely tolerable.

To the rest of the country, it was Independence Day, four years after the end of the Civil War. But to Newporters, it was Ida Lewis Day. Ida's name and fame had spread at a surprising speed for the nineteenth century. It was almost ironic that on an island largely inhabited by summer cottagers and the well-to-do, it would be a plain, modest laborer who drew all the attention. With this added local significance, more than the usual number came out to the waterfront to enjoy the holiday festivities, which included a fine parade and plenty of Ida admirers. Among the other concessions available were 'Ida-

This popular portrait shows Ida with a scarf worn fichu *style.*
Harper's Weekly *replicated this pose in a cover illustration.*

wise' paraphernalia. Boys wore hats and ties, while girls
donned scarves emblazoned with Ida's name. Girls modeled
their scarf fashion after the one Ida wore *fichu* style (in a knot
off to one side) in a photo taken by Manchester Brothers of
Providence, which had been widely circulated.

The etchings of her in *Harper's* and *Leslie's* helped give the
world an idea of what this mighty heroine looked like. In
truth, Ida's frame was no more than that of average female
height for the day, neither short nor tall. She was slim—her
weight a mere 103 pounds. Her size alone made the stories of
her rescues even more sensational. Her facial demeanor was
pleasant and her strong features and clear hazel eyes were
wide-set and framed by brown hair. It never seemed to gray
even as she aged. If she smiled just right, there were dimples
in each cheek. But in every photograph and portrait, she was
somber-faced.

Over 4,000 poured onto the streets of Newport that hot
Independence Day. All came to hear their homegrown, hometown heroine speak.

They would be sadly disappointed. Unaccustomed and
awkward in the role of *cause celebre,* Ida was acutely embarrassed by the attention and far too shy to speak before a large
crowd. Even in private she redirected conversations about her
rescues to instead talk about the lighthouse, the harbor, the
weather, or her family.

At the core a simple Yankee woman, she would never truly
feel comfortable with the suffocating attention lavished upon
her. Over time, she merely came to a point of begrudging
acceptance and tolerance regarding her fame. To her way of
thinking, her acts of rescue were just part of the job, and
nothing that anyone else wouldn't do if given the same set of
circumstances. So it was peculiar to her that society would
make such a big deal out of merely doing one's job.

Of her heroic deeds, she said, "If there were some people

out there who needed help, I would get into my boat and go to them even if I knew I couldn't get back. Wouldn't you?"

So it was on what must have been an overwhelming Independence Day, that twenty-seven-year-old Ida mustered up the courage to nervously participate in the events that included a formal presentation of a new lifesaving rowboat, aptly christened the *Rescue.*

The boat was a heavy, long thing: fourteen feet in length, two feet-four inches in breadth and sixteen inches deep, constructed of cedar, white oak, and black walnut. The coxswain board was crafted from the latter wood, with a pure white finish and gilt stripe all around. All the fastenings were of wrought copper, with not a particle of iron. The cushions were deep red and plush, and the oars—four of them—a heavy walnut. The cost was estimated to be upward of $250. The boat was paid for by subscription, with a number of dignitaries, including newly elected President Ulysses S. Grant, contributing to its manufacture.

After the handsome boat was paraded through the streets several times on wheels, it stopped at Washington Square. There it was formally presented to Ida by Francis Brindley, former president of the Boston Common Council and a scholar of the classics.

"This boat has none of the glitter and pretense of the silver-oared barge of Cleopatra, which floated on the Cydnus like a burnished throne; but it comes to you rich in artistic skill and treighted [treated] with the kindest wishes of the inhabitants of Newport," said Brindley with a flourish. "On behalf of the donors, and as their honored representative, I commit it to your care, knowing how well and wisely it will be used and managed by the Heroine of Lime Rock, whose name and exploits will be preserved by tradition so long as any portion of the shores of Rhode Island shall be washed by the waters of Narragansett."

An illustration from Leslie's Illustrated Newspaper *featuring Ida in the* Rescue *after the dedication ceremony on July 4, 1869.*

While the historical reference might have been lost on Ida, the attention surely was not. Flustered, she acknowledged the gesture, but declined to take center stage. In her stead, Colonel Thomas Wentworth Higginson, a well-known feminist and abolitionist at the time, addressed the throng and accepted the vessel on her behalf.

"I am requested by Miss Lewis to return thanks in her name to the donors, and to the citizens of Newport. Miss Lewis desires me to say that she never has made a speech in her life and she doesn't expect to begin now," he said.

"She receives the boat with pleasure not alone as an earnest representation of the good feeling of her fellow citizens, but also as a means of doing a little more hereafter, if the occasion should come, in the same direction. She has fortunately learned to do what the proverb recommends as the height of wisdom, to paddle her own canoe. She will endeavor to paddle this one, and if any of you should be so unfortunate as to get into difficulty in the neighborhood of Lime Rock, so long as you can see this boat riding at anchor there, it will say to you as boys sometimes say to a playmate who has fallen, 'Come here and I will pick you up.' Much has been said about her services in this direction. When she performed this duty she had no thought of its being recognized. In fact, I believe if she thought what men would say about it, probably the act never would have been done at all.

"Miss Lewis is grateful to you for your acknowledgment of what seemed to her a simple act of duty; and she is more grateful to Divine Providence which enabled her to do what she hopes never to have to do again."

The rescue of the two soldiers from Fort Adams had been a result of their own inebriation, a common occurrence along the waterfront of Newport as in many harbor towns of the time where bars and saloons were plentiful. The temperance movement was in full swing in the late 1800s, and had many followers. As a Christian, Ida eschewed excesses in general, and knew firsthand how alcohol had precipitated many of the near-drowning incidents on her watch.

"The thought of the dangers that men have undergone in these waters is to her a more serious thing than any praises she has received for helping them," he continued, making poetic reference to the recurring problem of alcoholism among soldiers and sailors alike, and Ida's involvement in the temperance movement. "There is many a sailor who has passed the Lime Rock safely, to be ruined by the grog shops of Newport. And when she is aiding in the temperance cause, Miss Lewis is doing a work that will last after the last plank of this boat has been dashed in pieces on the rocks. Or mouldered away on the shore."

But the presentations weren't over. Ida was presented with an elegant yoke made of rosewood with a solid silver mounting, silver sockets, and a crimson cord and tassel. It read:

Presented to Miss Ida Lewis
by the Narragansett Boat Club
Providence, July 1869

"Upon a solitary rock surrounded by the sea is alone dwelling," began William Sheffield upon presenting the pricey gift. He launched into a flowery, long-winded speech, recounting the heroic event that brought Ida to Newport's attention. "That young girl with resolute purpose and steady nerve pushed her yawl afloat and with practiced arm guided it over the frothing sea to the wreck of a craft which was unable to contend with the elements."

He waxed poetic, obscuring the facts somewhat and neglecting to mention brother Hosea's role in the rescue. He ended with a flourish.

"Her efforts were not for gain. Her high daring was not for sale. The consciousness following upon duty performed was the only reward she sought, and the sweet satisfaction of that poor girl for one short hour as she exulted over the lives she had saved was above the realization of the dreams of ambition by statesmen and warriors, and such as the combined wealth of the Barrings and Rothschilds could not purchase."

The heat of the day, coupled with the realization that it would be difficult to top a speech like that, resulted in a brief third presentation. The officers from the steamer Newport simply thanked her when handing her their gift of silk flags to fly on her new vessel.

After copious thanks all around, Higginson bid them farewell on Ida's behalf. The audience gave three cheers for

Ida and broke into applause as she stepped into the boat and had her picture taken.

Later that day, a crowd of 1,000 assembled at the waterfront on Long Wharf to watch her launch her new skiff across the narrow passageway to Lime Rock. It was three o'clock in the afternoon, when Ida, dressed in a black gown and a red Garibaldi sack fastened by a leather belt around her waist, stepped into the vessel. It was a far cry from her weather-worn skiff, and the oars felt strangely heavy in her grasp. Rowing being a chore for which she was well accustomed, her new fans watched as she gently slid the oars into the water. Amid cheers and the waving of handkerchiefs, a cannon boomed in her honor as she steered the craft through the crowded harbor. The shy, uncomfortable Ida had disappeared and another one emerged, filled with confidence and assurance. She struck out with bold, easy strokes, moving the weight of the boat effortlessly through the still surface of the water, as if endowed with the strength of a man. She steered the small rescue vessel toward Lime Rock, around the other sailboats. She then slowly turned to the cheering spectators on shore and smiled, as she lifted her arm into the air, waving a small white handkerchief in acknowledgment.

She was at ease now. The day was behind her, she was out of the limelight, and she was going home to her safe, beloved light. But whether she realized it or not, life as she had known it had been inextricably altered. She was no longer just the lighthouse keeper's daughter. She had become, much against her will, the heroine of Lime Rock.

Chapter 2
In the Beginning

Ida knows how to handle a boat. She can hold one to wind'ard in a gale better than any man I ever saw, wet an oar, and yes, do it too, when the sea is breaking over her.
  —Thomas Rudolph Lewis, Ida's brother

Ida was born of the sea. She loved everything about it. At a young age, she was drawn to it. It was more than just splashing in the waves of coastal Newport; she took to swimming early on and was considered a strong swimmer. Her energy and strength set her apart from her peers, and it was known that she could handle a boat with more skill than any boy her age. A true tomboy, Ida enjoyed being outdoors and spent an inordinate amount of time outside. As she grew in size and age, she often rowed about the harbor for her own pleasure, and took time to help other boaters if they needed it. She was twelve when her father accepted the appointment

Ida Lewis posed often in a rowboat. Here, she is photographed in her reliable skiff.

as lighthouse keeper and she took great pleasure in accompanying him on his sojourns to the light.

Captain Hosea Lewis rowed the 220 yards from the Newport shore to the cluster of limestone ledges known as Lime Rock twice daily when he took over the responsibilities of lighthouse keeper. He and his family lived in town, in the house where Ida was born.

In the 1800s, keepers in general were appointed from amongst the ranks of mariners—men who had knowledge of the sea and the changing weather. They were expected to be able to read cloud formations, wind directions, and changes in tides without sophisticated nautical equipment. They were also expected to give assistance to shipwrecked seamen.

Lime Rock is but a cluster of rocks set deep in Newport harbor—a series of limestone ledges which, before being discovered as a key location for a lighthouse, had been excavated by Newport builders for centuries. As early as 1712, well before Newport became a growing port, according to the records of minutes taken at the town's quarterly meeting, Mr.

Anthony Young was granted permission to excavate lime from the rocks. Lime was used in the mixing of cement, and the lime from Lime Rocks was considered especially durable.

As the harbor flourished and changed, so did the need for navigational aids, including the placement of lighthouses and light ships. In fact, a light boat (in essence a floating lighthouse) had been established in the Narragansett Bay area in the early 1800s. And makeshift beacons were sometimes put along the shore to guide ships and boats safely into port. The beacons were sometimes nothing more than large bonfires or barrels of flammable pitch to help outline the coastline. They were, however, easily imitated by pirates and other unscrupulous characters who lured unsuspecting or inexperienced navigators to abandoned stretches of beach where they were looted.

The problem of pirates and looters was prolific, as was that of smugglers, so much so that the Revenue Marine was organized in 1790 to guard against it. This service was later called the Revenue Cutter Service—the precursor to the U.S. Coast Guard—for which Hosea Lewis worked as a pilot, captaining his own cutter. In addition, lighthouses were becoming an increasingly important maritime priority.

Until the late 1700s, there were only a dozen lighthouses in the country, but they were built and maintained by local governments. Around the same time that the Revenue Marine was established, the federal government created the Bureau of Lighthouses in 1789. By the turn of the century, there were two dozen lighthouses in service up and down the Atlantic Coast. By the time Lime Rock light was built, the country had moved into high gear with lighthouse construction. To keep tighter control over the ever-expanding operations, a Lighthouse Board was organized in 1852, which would end up supervising lighthouses for the next fifty-eight years. It fell under the duties of the Secretary of the Treasury—who was also president of the Board—to discharge administrative duties relating to lighthouses and other aids of navigation, and to sanction appointments. The coast was then divided into twelve lighthouse districts, each one assigned to an army or navy inspector. It was this new board that set the ball in motion for the building of the Lime Rock "light-station."

By the 1800s, Newport had grown into a resort community. The island on the southeastern tip of Rhode Island had originally been established in 1639 by a group of religious refugees from Massachusetts. By colonial times, its placement in the Atlantic Ocean made Newport an ideal port for the triangular trade of molasses, rum, and slaves, linking it to Africa and the West Indies. But the American Revolution and embargo from the War of 1812 crippled the economy, which proved to be a turning point for the city. Skipped over by the industrial revolution that was feeding the thriving economies of the eastern seaboard, Newport transformed itself into a vacation destination. By the 1840s it was an established summer colony for wealthy New Yorkers, sort of a predecessor to the Gilded Age that would be ushered in later that century. Boston intellectuals, artisans, poets, writers, and thinkers soon followed, attracted by the island's rustic setting and quiet simplicity.

The Civil War had also introduced a new element to Newport, for it brought with it a strong military presence. The Navy moved its naval academy there for four years before moving it out again. What remained was the Naval War College, which moved in the 1880s, and of course, Fort Adams, which would play a crucial role in the years to come for Ida Lewis.

The first Fort Adams had been built originally in 1799, as an open, irregularly shaped fortification to hold approximately twenty guns. It was situated along what was then known as Brenton's Point, a small peninsula that jutted out and hooked around from Newport Harbor, almost pointing to Lime Rock. Named after President John Adams, the fort was part of a

series of beefed-up fortifications that came in the wake of the
Revolutionary War, when British troops easily seized control
of Newport. Above the archway of the opening gateway was a
stone tablet inscribed: Fort Adams, *The Rock on Which the
Storm Will Beat.* The inscription referred to the oncoming
winds of the War of 1812. The war never hit coastal Rhode
Island, and Fort Adams never saw any action, but a wave of
concern prompted by the burning of Washington (due to
feeble coastal defenses) by then-president James Monroe
spurred a second and then a third wave of fortification construction and reconstruction along the coast. Fort Adams
was earmarked for the latter.

Congress appropriated $50,000 for the project, and Lieu-
tenant Colonel Joseph Totten moved to Newport to supervise
it. Considered the premier military architect and engineer of
his day, Totten stayed in Newport while the fort was under
reconstruction until 1838, when he was appointed Chief of
Engineers of the United States Army. At a quarterly town
meeting it was recorded that in 1831, Colonel Totten "took
stone from Lime Rock. The U.S. government had to pay
twelve cents a cask of the easternmost part of the island but
nothing from the westernmost part." Totten was using the
limestone to make cement for the rebuilding of the fortification. The fort was built as a massive work with structural walls
constructed of local shale, as well as bricks from clay obtained
in Rhode Island and granite shipped by schooner from Maine.
Since so much raw material was needed to complete the massive structure, Totten constantly advertised in the *Newport
Mercury* for New England contractors who could provide
what would end up being millions of locally-made bricks.

The magnitude of a fort was determined by the size of the
garrison, its length in perimeter, and strength of artillery. Fort
Adams, while never fully armed or garrisoned, was designed
to accommodate a peacetime garrison of 200, and war com-

plement of 2,400 with 468 mounted cannon. Its perimeter stretched to almost 1,800 yards, making the fort one of the largest in the country. While the fort was never attacked, its shape was considered very different at the time, employing an irregular pentagon shape.

Finally finished in 1857 at a cost of $3 million, Fort Adams was completed the same year Lime Rock Lighthouse was finished, and Hosea Lewis moved his family out into the harbor.

Lime Rock had been commissioned by an act of Congress in 1853 and $1,000 was appropriated to build the crude, stubby stone tower which housed the lantern (which Lewis dubbed "the sentry box"). A small wooden shanty was built next to it, in case foul weather forced Lewis to stay on the island. It was completed the next year. Like many of the early lighthouses, the original Lime Rock tower only had a beacon. Early ones consisted of nothing more than an oil-burning lantern encased in a wooden or iron frame with thick panes of glass. Oftentimes, they had solid wicks and were suspended by iron chains from the top of the lantern. They burned fish or whale oil, which needed to be replenished two or three times a night, and threw a small light. Lime Rock was built after the introduction of the Fresnel lens, which created a much brighter, focused beam that could be seen far from the harbor entry.

Work on the lighthouses was not only costly, it was hazardous and backbreaking. A crew of laborers was hired to build the stone tower. One of them was Hosea Lewis' son from his first marriage, Joseph Stockbridge Lewis. The crew had neither steam nor electric power. They relied on their own physical strength to haul and lift the huge stones, mix the mortar, and carry other building materials and supplies, all of which had to be transported by boat to the small island of limestone.

Following the months he was employed helping to build the original light, Joseph was appointed the first lighthouse keeper, but left the position after six months. His father had been a pilot for twelve years aboard a revenue cutter, but had been forced to retire early because of his poor health—namely, a bad heart. He gladly took over the position.

The salary for a lighthouse keeper was $350 per year, and Hosea Lewis accepted the appointment for this sum. The forty-nine-year-old Lewis was appointed on November 5, 1853, and began his twice-a-day trek to the small tower, often bringing his constant companion, young Ida, with him to fill, set, and extinguish the light. Her half-brother Joseph, the previous lighthouse keeper at Lime Rock, left Newport to move to New Bedford, Massachusetts, where he married.

Hosea Lewis was originally from Hingham, Massachusetts. Following the death of his first wife (the mother of Joseph), he and second wife Idawalley Zoradia Wiley married on March 17, 1838, in Newport. His wife was originally from New Shoreham, Rhode Island, the daughter of Dr. A. C. Wiley. Their first child was a boy named Horatio, who died from unknown causes at the age of ten in 1854, three years before his father received the appointment. The next in the lineage was a daughter, Idawalley Zoradia, her mother's namesake. Known simply as Ida*, she was born February 25, 1842. By the time her father took on his new job, she had been taught all the skills that would have been imparted to her older brother had he lived. She quickly mastered the oars and the rudder, and could soon skipper the small boat like an expert seaman.

As a cutter pilot, Lewis' life had been hardened by the sea.

---

* Over time, as was more common than not, misprints in city records, including Ida's own marriage certificate, inadvertently dropped the letter "i" out of the last syllable of her middle name, leaving her name to be remembered through history as Idawalley Zorada. To underscore this problem with early record keeping, even her mother's death record was recorded incorrectly as "Ida Doradia," and her parents' own marriage certificate states her name as "Serada."

He was no stranger to the constant prospect and probability of sacrificing his own life to rescue others during the course of duty. It was Hosea Lewis who taught Ida how to rescue a drowning man. Countless trips back and forth from the small pier known as Jones Wharf to the lighthouse island were filled with talk of his years on the open ocean as a cutter pilot. It was dangerous, grueling work. When appointed to the position of keeper, the man who appointed him noted that Lewis had proven himself over the length of his career, as he was considered by his superiors to be impeccably honest and above reproach. It was her father that instilled in Ida the seed of heroism.

Over the course of these trips, Ida grew into a seasoned, powerful oarswoman. With time and experience, she developed an innate feel for the boat and composure on the sea. Lewis had already educated her on the fundamentals of taking care of the light, should the need arise.

Lewis had to tend the light while living in downtown Newport, on the corner of Spring and Brewer Streets. But the frequent rowing to and from Lime Rock began to take its toll on Lewis and his health. For three years, he and his family lived in Newport, near the harbor. After several requests to the Lighthouse Board that it would be much more practical for him live on the island, the matter was resolved.

"This is a matter of difficulty during the winter storms and would in some cases be quite impracticable. It seems desirable, on other accounts, that the keeper should live on the spot. That he may do so, a house is necessary, as the present building is but a temporary shanty." Thus wrote the Superintendent of Lights in an 1856 report. In August of that year, Congress allocated another $1,500 to build a "keeper's dwelling." A year later, the Lewis family finally moved into the new home on June 29, 1857. The *Newport Mercury* reported: "One would suppose there was hardly room to

A postcard of Lime Rock Lighthouse, c. late 1800s.

swing a cat on the lime rocks and yet a spot large enough has been found for a commodious two-story brick house with ample space in front, and barring that it is a little rough and irregular for a lawn, with a walk leading to the lighthouse and the little beach where the keeper hauls his boat."

Not only did Keeper Lewis have a new home, the following month his salary was increased to $560 a year. Unfortunately, his good luck was short-lived. Lewis suffered a debilitating stroke in October, just four months after the move to Lime Rock. It rendered him partially paralyzed and completely unable to fulfill his duties as keeper. After several months of convalescence, he recovered enough to walk with the aid of a cane, but spent much of his time sitting in a chair. More than once, he watched helplessly from a window as his daughter took her life in her hands. He eventually deteriorated to the point that he had to be constantly cared for and even fed by family members.

When Hosea Lewis fell ill, his wife Zoradia and young Ida shared his duties. The brunt of the hard labor fell to the fifteen year old. Even though she was a girl, Ida was still a full five years older than her next younger brother, Thomas Rudolph (referred to by the family as "Rud"). Already finished with formal schooling, Ida put her expert rowing skills to good use, ferrying her three younger siblings to and from shore to attend school each day. Along with Rud, there was her brother Hosea and sister Harriet.

Her father watched nervously from his chair perched near the kitchen window. "Again and again, have I seen the children from the window as they were returning from school in some heavy blow, when Ida alone was with them, and old sailor that I am, I felt that I would not give a penny for their lives, so furious was the storm—yes sir. I have watched them 'til I could not bear to look any longer, expecting every moment to see them swamped and the crew at the mercy of the waves, and then I have turned away and said to my wife— let me know if they get safe in, for I could not endure to see them perish and realize that we were powerless to save them. And oh you cannot tell the relief when she cried out: they have got safe to the rock, Father. It was a mighty weight off my mind, I can assure you. I have seen Ida in the bitter winter weather obliged to cut off her frozen stockings at the knees."

As is the case with many heroes, her early life helped shape Ida for her future role. Her family responsibilities and ease in a boat seemed to reinforce Ida's natural inclinations and quick thinking in times of danger. Yet her uncommon perseverance and fearlessness were undoubtedly part of her character, and uniquely her own. Although she was never formally trained in lifesaving—save some pointers passed on to her by her father—Ida's instincts, Yankee practicality, and coolheadedness would come to her aid again and again in future rescues.

She was obviously the strongest and most dependable member of her family, and well-loved and respected by them. Her brother Rud, also a sailor, often praised his sister's valor and skills. "Ida knows how to handle a boat. She can hold one to wind'ard in a gale better than any man I ever saw, wet an oar, and yes, do it too, when the sea is breaking over her."

Those skills would soon come into play, in a manner that none of the Lewis family would have been able to predict.

Chapter 3
The First Rescue

We have only one life to live, and when our time comes we've got to go; so it doesn't matter how. I never thought of danger when people needed help. At such times you're busy thinking of other things.

—Ida Lewis

Newport was still decades away from its heyday, the Gilded Age, which was marked by opulence and ostentatious extravagance, as evidenced by the construction of massive estates costing more than Fort Adams itself. The island of Aquidneck had drawn to its shores the wealthy far before the names Astor or Vanderbilt graced its streets. Affluent southerners and Caribbean planters came to vacation during the summer months, anxious to leave the oppressive heat and humidity of Dixie and the islands. The expansive white shores and ever-present gentle breezes were a major attraction.

They were followed by the Bostonian aristocrats, and a wave of esthetes: artists, writers, poets, and thinkers, who were attracted to the rustic nature of the untouched island and wanted to escape from notoriety. New Yorkers had discovered Newport, but there was no direct route to travel there easily. There was also a lack of summer housing, with hotels being the primary means of vacationing. Most of Aquidneck was still pastoral, with tracts of land still being parceled in large blocks as farmland. Even if someone wanted to buy a smaller lot and build a summer cottage, there were few available.

Real estate development proved to be the key to the boon in Newport in the mid-1800s. Until 1845, land had been packaged as cultivating property. That changed dramatically under the auspices of Alfred Smith, a realtor with a vision. He started packaging land for real estate development and, with two other men, bought three hundred acres of farmland bordering downtown Newport. They subdivided the lots, streets were laid out on a grid, and they planted trees. Values increased overnight.

The land-developing move coincided with the introduction of the first overnight steamship between New York and the island. The ship was part of the Fall River Line under the control of Jim Fisk, entrepreneur and controversial businessman. Travel to and from the island became convenient, tourism boomed, and the hotels filled up. Anticipating the crush of new tourists, a six hundred-bed hotel called Ocean House was built. Eventually, those repeat vacationers became renters and then cottage-builders. The time came when wooden summer cottages began to dot the shores, a precursor to the marble giants to come.

Thanks to the same publications that made Ida a household word—*Harper's* and *Leslie's*—Newport was becoming popular and the world began to view the ocean port as a fine vacation spot. A new "highway"—Bellevue Avenue—was developed, which looped the oceanfront and offered sweeping views. It would soon be home to many of the famous Newport mansions. One of the earliest was Chateau Sur Mer, whose owner was William Shephard Wetmore. His son, George Peabody Wetmore, went on to become a U.S. Senator. Newport was now on its way. But along with the influx of the well-to-do summer visitors were those who lived and worked in Newport. Organizations began to spring up, appealing to those Newporters of lineage and breeding, including the Newport Historical Society, Newport Reading Room, and Newport Gaslight Society. Newport had its own aristocracy who would later blend with the multi-millionaires from New York society.

On September 4, 1858, Ida had her first brush with this fine Newport stock. She was sixteen, about the same age as the four boys she was about to rescue. The boys came from privileged families, who would have had no reason to meet Ida or her family if it hadn't been for the strange fate that brought them together on that late afternoon. Having moved to Lime Rock two years before, Ida had already proven herself a capable oarswoman and fine swimmer, as well as a vigilant observer of the harbor around her.

On an end-of-summer day, four boys of local Newport's class of privilege would take one last jaunt on a friend's boat, and wind up being saved by a lowly lighthouse keeper's daughter.

It started out as a simple, easy adventure that Samuel Cambrelang Powell and three of his private school classmates set out in a catboat (a small pleasure sailboat)—the Hug-'Em-Snug—to have a picnic on a small rocky island formation known then as "the Dumplings." The island was well past Lime Rock, situated further out in the wide end of the harbor, closer to Fort Adams. A large stone cylindrical fortress had been built on the island, and was used as a shooting target for

the nearby fort. After finishing their lunch, they re-boarded
the vessel and sailed out of the mouth of the harbor, joining
the other sleek sailboats and pleasure craft that had accumu-
lated on the waves.

As the day drew to a close, they headed back to shore and
into the inner harbor. They were soon passing between Lime
Rock and Fort Adams, trying to catch the northwesterly wind
for which the harbor was known. Clouds had moved in, and
the cover hanging overhead chilled the September afternoon,
making it unseasonably cool for that time of year. Dusk was
starting to settle on the water, and the threat of darkness was
fast approaching. The boys dropped sail, and decided to let
the tide carry them toward Jones Wharf. The boat lulled
against the rocking waves as it lazily moved toward the harbor.

Ida heard the laughter of the boys as they drew past the
lighthouse. They started to get a little rowdy, and she looked
up, watching the boys wrestle and joke. Perhaps to throw a
little adventure into the sail, or maybe to throw a little fear
into his fellow classmates, one of them—Theodore Wheaton
King (a son of a distinguished Newport physician)—jumped
up with a push. He dashed past Powell, Lance DeJongh (the
son of a retired naval lieutenant), and another boy, whose last
name was Smith but whose first is lost to time. He quickly
scrambled to the mast and shimmied to the top. His movement had the expected effect of creating a pitching motion.

As the small boat rocked back and forth, the danger of
the situation seemed to initially elude the four. The rocking
made the small boat take on water, and the boys began to
shout as they tried to steady it.

But it was too late. The swaying mast and King's weight
caused the vessel to capsize. The mast slipped under and the
hull turned upward toward the sky. Yelling for help, they
attempted to cling to the hull of the overturned boat, but
there were too many of them. They took turns two at a time

hanging onto the cold slippery hull, but spent more time treading water.

This was Ida's first recorded rescue. She had been watching the small sailboat move by Lime Rock, and was alarmed when King started his hijinks, certain the boat would topple over. She raced to her small skiff, and rowed swiftly out to the four boys, who were by this time gripped with fear. On shore, her father had managed to hobble to the window, and used his telescope to watch the rescue.

By the time she reached them, the hull was so slippery and small that they were forced to tread water to stay afloat. With temperatures dropping and their clothes weighing them down, two of the boys started to go under, their legs cramping.

Ida reached the spot, and was quickly able to haul the four in one by one. Her father collapsed into his chair after she managed to get the last one, drenched and shivering, safely into her boat.

"It was my father who showed me how to take people into my boat," explained Ida. "You have to draw them over the stern or they will tip you over. Sometimes they have caught hold of the gunwale, and then I have to make them let go until I can get them around to the stern."

By the time Ida reached Lime Rock with her cargo, Samuel Powell was unconscious. Her mother quickly mixed together molasses toddies, and handed out warm blankets to dry off the survivors. Powell was administered stimulants to help him regain consciousness. Once revived, he gushed his appreciation to Ida for her heroics.

But the four were embarrassed by the circumstances surrounding the rescue and feared punishment from their prominent parents, so they never told their families what actually happened. In fact, the incident was never discussed in at least one family until eleven years later when Ida was the object of a public love affair. She said herself that she didn't think the whole matter was worth talking about and never gave it another thought.*

Within two years of the rescue, King and DeJongh had enlisted in Company F, First Rhode Island volunteers. King was mortally wounded at Bull Run, where he was left on the field only to be found later by his father; he died shortly afterward. DeJongh returned from the war to Rhode Island, where he lived until his death in 1908. Smith, the lad with the unknown first name, died on a battlefield in Tunis. And Samuel C. Powell outlived Ida, serving as a pallbearer at her funeral in 1911.

For Ida, and the rest of her family, the rescue was forgotten, and would remain that way for more than a decade, when once again fate would intervene.

---

* A newspaper brief appeared years later in 1898, well into Ida's era of popularity. Someone noticed a man purchasing an Ida Lewis souvenir spoon for his wife, a gift for their wedding anniversary. When asked why, he sheepishly told the society reporter that he had been rescued by her in 1858, and owed his life—and hence his marriage—to her.

Chapter 4
The Summer of '69

She, who seldom went beyond the limits of her native city, became a citizen of the world—her name, a household treasure because she kept the light shining and feared not the duty perilous.

— Reverend W.C. Geisler, eulogist for Ida Lewis

It was the summer of 1869. Women would finally be given a voice in the political system, albeit a small one, by being granted the right to vote in the Territory of Wyoming. And while it would take another fifty years to have the Constitution amended to extend that right to *all* American women, the fight was under way a century before. As a movement, suffragettes were as committed as abolitionists before the Civil War. "The only question to be settled now is: Are women persons?" asked Susan B. Anthony rhetorically.

In the very year that Ida was being celebrated for her unparalleled act of bravery, Susan B. Anthony and Elizabeth Cady Stanton founded the National Woman Suffrage Association.

And with the country in the throes of admiring Ida, what better place than Newport to host a women's rights convention to "awaken thought among a new class of people" (as *The Revolution* stated in September 1869*)?

On August 27, the day after the 1869 convention, Stanton, Anthony, and several others set out on a boat ride to finally meet the woman who had matched men on the field of bravery. On that vessel was Colonel Higginson, who had spoken on behalf of Ida at the July 4th festivities. In that speech, Higginson, a feminist and abolitionist, had also made reference to the women's suffrage movement.

"She [Ida] has worked out the problem of women's rights in a different manner," the colonel told the crowd. "She has been accustomed to assuming the right of helping her fellow men without asking any questions." Ida never drew gender lines about her abilities. In truth, she eschewed any comparison to men in terms of her strength or bravery, and was reluctant to become a flag-bearer for the women's rights movement.

Cady recounted the boat ride in the newspaper she and Anthony published out of New York, *Revolution*. She glibly took sexist shots at the other male companions on the sailboat, who among others included a practitioner of phrenology, who examined Ida's head for his own article.

"It is touching to see how easily such gifted men in their hours of ease with songs, anecdotes, wit, and repartee, can condescend to commune with those who, according to our state constitutions, are the political equals of idiots, lunatics, and paupers.

"The home of Ida Lewis is on a high broken pile of rocks that dazzle the eye in the bright sunlight with their sparkling whiteness . . . Although our young heroine was busy at the

---

* *The Revolution,* September 2, 1869, vol. IV, no. 9.

washtub, she promptly made her appearance, apologizing for her dress. She said she was obliged to work and had so many visitors that she could not always be dressed to receive them.

"Just now Ida Lewis is the fashion. No one thinks of visiting Newport without seeing her. In one day she told us she had three hundred calls. She is a frail-looking girl, seemingly with but little force or endurance. She has a marked, pleasant face, light brown hair, hazel eyes, and a chin like Anna Dickinson . . . . We talked of the race between the Harvards and the Oxfords and all spoke hopefully of the time when girls, too, should enter the lists for the prizes of life."

Ida told her visitors about the rescue and of her rowing as a young girl, honing her skills to handle a boat adeptly and save so many.

"I rather think those men whose lives she saved were glad to see her *out of her sphere* that dark eventful day. Imagine those men saved by her skill and magnanimity seated in her quiet home, warmed and fed by her loving charity, safe from danger, fully reinstated in the normal condition of ordinary manhood, holding forth to her on 'woman's place,' 'her inferiority,' 'her subject condition in nature' . . . What multitudes of men are strutting up and down the highways of life, prating of their lordly gifts to reign and rule, who have been fished up from the Stygian pools of ignorance, disease and vice, and their feet placed on solid ground by the heroism and self-sacrifices of woman, who today sneer at the idea of her holding a ballot."

During the meeting, one thing was abundantly clear to the visitors.

"Ida Lewis is a girl of rare common sense and self-respect. She is modest, unaffected, and seems surprised rather than pleased with the amount of attention she is just now receiving."*

Ida handed Anthony and Cady photographs of herself, which she autographed, and saw them to their boat. When the sailboat *Catherine* shoved off, Ida breathed a sigh of relief. The meeting had been taxing upon her, perhaps because of the political nature of the women and their zeal for their cause. Ida later expressed her exasperation regarding the meeting, commenting that she would have rather conducted another rescue than a visit with Anthony and her companions.

At this point, it was little wonder that Ida agreed to have Colonel George D. Brewerton, a journalist, write what she would endorse as the official accounting of her life to date. Perhaps she was getting tired of repeating it herself. The clamor for information and for "everything Ida" descended upon her oppressively. The small sixty-six-page book, *Ida Lewis, The Heroine of Lime Rock*, was published in October of that year in the wake of the public furor over Ida. In its flyleaf, she testifies to its accuracy, but throughout, Brewerton asserts that even Ida had a hard time recalling the dates of the previous rescues, and rarely remembered the names or followed up on what later happened to those she saved.

A posed photo taken by Manchester Brothers in 1869 following the publication of Brewerton's biography of Ida.

"His [Brewerton's] account of the Rescues and other matters connected with my history and parentage are truly

told, the particulars having been furnished by myself," Ida
wrote. "I commend this book to those who may be curious to
know more of my life and antecedents, as a faithful record
and the only one I have authorized to be given."

It was also in this flurry of publicity that Ida was to
receive her first taste of celebrity. It must have come as a
shock to Ida when she opened the letter from the Life Saving
Benevolent Association of New York to find a check for $100,
and a carefully wrapped package containing a Moroccan red,
velvet-lined case. Upon lifting the heavy silver medal out of
the handsome case, Ida read the inscription: "Presented to
Miss Ida Lewis as a testimonial to her skill, courage, and
humanity in rescuing two men from drowning in the harbor of
Newport, R.I. during a severe storm on the 29th of March."

Ida obviously knew where New York was, as the inspector
for the 3rd Lighthouse District (to whom she reported) was
located on Staten Island. But she had never been there,
although she would come close when she married the next year.

The Life Saving Benevolent Association of New York was
founded in 1848 by a group of prominent merchants, ship
owners, and underwriters who realized the need to establish a
system for saving lives. The loss of lives was tragic but also
costly, especially to shipping company owners and insurance
companies underwriting the ventures. The Life Saving
Benevolent Association of New York was thus born, which in
part created a reward system to encourage the salvage of lives
along the lower eastern coast near New Jersey and Long
Island, New York.

The organization asked for and received from Congress
and the Secretary of the Treasury $10,000 as an appropria-
tion. Its mission was "to recognize and reward courage, skill,
and seamanship displayed in the rescue of human life on the
sea or any navigable waters . . . and to award medals, medal
pins, and sums of money for life saving, to encourage training

in seamanship, lifeboat work, methods of rescue in the water, and the resuscitation of victims of submersions, and to perform such other services of benevolence."

Ida never applied for the award, or even knew that she was being considered. The impact of having received her first medal and what was then a sizable sum of money must have been overwhelming. It set the tone for the rest of the summer. Accolades kept coming.

It was several weeks later, at the end of May 1869, that the Rhode Island General Assembly passed a resolution honoring Ida Lewis, the first such governmental recognition for this daughter of the lighthouse keeper. In a missive accompanying the ornate parchment resolution, John Bartlett, then-secretary of state of Rhode Island, expressed the state's gratitude to the twenty-seven year old. "I take pleasure in transmitting to you a resolution unanimously adopted by the General Assembly of this state at its late session in Newport acknowledging your valuable services in saving so many lives from drowning."

The document, complete with gold seal, read:

> *Resolved: That this General Assembly desires to recognize officially the heroism of Miss Ida Lewis, of Newport, in repeatedly saving the lives of drowning men, at the risk of her own and we are proud that one of our own citizens, by her courage and humanity, has won admiration of the whole country.*

Less than two weeks later, another honor arrived when Major General Henry Hunt, then the commanding officer of the 5th Regiment U.S. Artillery and the Garrison of Fort Adams, sent a letter to Ida. Included with the note of thanks for saving Sergeant Adams and Private McCloughlin, was $218, contributed by the thankful officers and soldiers of the regiment. The fort also presented her with a gold watch following the rescue.

Within a whirlwind two months of newspaper publicity, the world finally woke up to the existence of a present-day heroine. Newport dedicated Independence Day to her. Ida was reeling. Given the times, it was a weighty matter for the town of Newport to dedicate that day. It was a mere four years after the end of the Civil War. Wounds had yet to heal, but parts of the country were still riding high on an euphoric sense of patriotism; a surge of nationalism was spreading through the eastern states. When July 4th rolled around, Ida was quite reluctant to be the center of attention, but obliged out of a sense of duty.

After receiving the beautiful new rowboat *Rescue,* Ida had nowhere to house it. Her own skiff was tied to a mooring on the edge of Lime Rock. The situation was rectified the next day. Among her stream of steady visitors during that summer was U.S. Customs Collector Seth Macy, a powerful man of the day, for Newport was a customs port and the collector's position—a political appointment—enjoyed a lofty status.

At that time, the nation was divided into customs collection districts. In each district there was a headquarters port with a customhouse. The customs district usually consisted of the headquarters port and subports within the district. The Customs Collection District of Newport, Rhode Island, consisted of Newport as the headquarters port and North Kingston, East Greenwich, Barrington, Warren, Bristol, and Westerly as ports of delivery. Some of the ports of delivery later became customs districts themselves. (In 1801, Bristol and Warren became a separate collection district and in 1842, Westerly and Stonington, Connecticut, were joined and became a separate district.)

The Collector of Customs was the chief officer of the district and was responsible for numerous tasks. Not only did he collect duties, keep records, and report financial transactions to the Secretary of the Treasury, he was also responsible for enforcing the revenue laws and for collecting fines and penalties for violation of those laws. The position also made him responsible for the documentation of American merchant vessels, the recording of the entrances and clearances of vessels within the district, and the administration of the customhouse. He was also the man accountable for the lighthouses within his district, and for the protection of American seamen and passengers on American vessels, as well as the revenue cutters within his district.

The Collectors of Customs were very influential federal officials. For most of the nineteenth century the customs service was the largest civil agency in the federal government. The collectors were in charge of the deputy collectors, the surveyors, inspectors, weighers, gaugers, and other customs employees within their districts; they also appointed these people. Therefore political patronage added to the powers of the collectors. It was through him that much of the information about Ida's rescues was filtered to key figures in the government.

On that day after Independence Day, accompanying Collector Macy were two highly controversial, very wealthy businessmen of the time: Jim Fisk and Jay Gould.

Fisk was the president of the Fall River Steamship Company, which was instrumental to the tourism boon. Gould had already gained a reputation as an unscrupulous businessman. Both of them were looked upon with great disdain, especially by the Vanderbilts, their archrivals. In the world of robber barons, there were the captains of industry of which Vanderbilt, Carnegie, and Rockefeller belonged, and then there were Jim Fisk and Jay Gould, who were absent any conscience and preyed upon weak businesses to develop their own empires.

But some say there was another side to the two. Perhaps there was a glimpse of it on that day in 1869, when upon stepping onto the island, Fisk noted that Ida had nowhere to house the glorious boat, so he ordered Macy to have a boathouse constructed at his own expense. He also had a silk pennant made for the *Rescue,* which Ida had framed and placed on the wall of her home. Jay Gould presented her with lavish gold oarlocks to accompany the boat. It would be but two months hence that the notorious twosome would attempt to control the U.S. gold market.

Meeting Fisk and Gould, and a host of others who comprised the class of very wealthy, very powerful, and very high-profiled figures of the day, added a new dimension to Ida's celebrity. Her instant fame was perhaps the hardest thing for Ida to grasp at this point, being generally uncomfortable with the attention. But to become the center of attention—to be instantly admired by those who existed at the very top of the class system in the late 1800s—that was quite a different story. Ida may not have realized the import of this attention.

Though she may not have ever heard of the Sorosis Society, it was in that month of July 1869 that she was made an honorary member of the elitist women's group, and was sent a gold engraved pin from the New York Chapter. The Sorosis Society was the premier women's group of the eighteenth century, modeled after male secret societies such as the Masons. Its primary function was as a literary group though it had the trappings of a volunteer organization.

Being made a member, honorary or otherwise, was most likely lost on Ida, who even if she had had the inclination and desire to read novels, had little time to do so. But Ida knew the importance of that pin. Later photographs and events often revealed her wearing it clasped at her neck or on her shoulder.

Ida made no pretense of culture. She was not educated in any formal sense; her schooling ended at fifteen when she and her family relocated to the island. Ida was not refined. She had traveled no further than the city limits of Newport, unless

A portrait of Ida in her early 50s. The gold pin at her neck was given to her by the Sorosis Society.

one defines the harbor as outside the city boundaries. Her life was very limited, and her understanding of society etiquette nonexistent.

But she would never have the chance to embarrass herself. That summer of 1869 was replete with throngs of visitors. As Ida herself said, "every Mrs. Astor and every Mrs. Vanderbilt and every Mrs. Belmont you ever heard of called on me with whole boatloads of men and women that all talked to me at once and treated me as if I were a kind of real queen."

But despite all the attention she received from the upper classes, she would never once be included on a guest list to any lavish affair. Not once did Ida have a glimpse of the inside of any of the oversized summer cottages or outrageous mansions. She was, at most, an attraction.

If Ida needed some time to deal with her own popularity, she wasn't afforded the luxury. That summer of 1869 alone, her father counted between 9,000 and 10,000 visitors who made the pilgrimage to Lime Rock to meet the heroine. On a given day, she was fond of telling reporters, she would shake upwards of 600 hands.

Some of the visitors were quite prestigious. Her most important one was undoubtedly Ulysses S. Grant. Inaugurated 18th President just months before, Grant was visiting

Newport and requested an interview with Ida. His schedule
was overbooked, so he asked Ida (through correspondence) if
she could row to shore and meet his entourage, which
included his wife.

As always, she obeyed. A nervous Ida dressed in her holiday attire used *Rescue* to row over to the meeting place at the
end of Long Wharf. She seldom used the new boat, preferring
her old skiff, called *Courageous Child of Columbia,* to it
instead. She was brought to the carriage where Grant was
waiting. The meeting was brief, but Grant expressed his great
pleasure at meeting a lady so distinguished in the field of
humanity. He told her, "I am happy to meet you, Miss Lewis,
as one of the heroic, noble women of the age." By some
reports, according to legend, Grant was so insistent on meeting Ida that he supposedly said, "I have come to see Ida
Lewis, and to see her I'd get wet up to my armpits if necessary." When asked what he did say to her, Ida shrugged it off,
as all flattering speeches sounded alike to her.

Other names tied with that summer and the subsequent
ones to follow included General William Tecumseh Sherman
and Admiral Dewey, who would visit often during his
appointment as Secretary of the Lighthouse Board. On his
first trip to Lime Rock, he told Ida, "Miss Lewis, I want to
smoke on your half-acre rock for a half-hour." They spent
many afternoons chatting easily while he smoked. When General Sherman arrived, he sat on the rock for "nearly an hour,
asking me questions about my life and saying he was glad to
get to such a peaceful place," Ida said.

As she herself would note, "There's hardly a great admiral
or noted general that hasn't been here to see me." Perhaps
men of noted bravery found in Ida what they found in themselves: the ability to act in the face of danger and great peril to
one's own safety.

She was particularly pleased with the comments of the

Secretary of the Treasury, George S. Boutwell (who served from 1869–1873). He came that summer to meet her and she delighted in telling the story of their encounter. "He said he came purposely to thank me personally for saving the life of a soldier from Fort Adams, because the light was in his department, and he was proud to have a woman in his department who was not finicky about getting her hair wet."

But all the visitors weren't famous. In fact, of the 9,000–10,000 admirers who supposedly came to meet her, only a few were. And they weren't always polite, either. A *Boston Journal* article that was published the following summer recounted the months following Ida's catapult to fame.

"Everybody thought Ida Lewis would be left in peace this season after the furor of last, the public soon tiring usually of such demonstrations but such is not likely to be the case. The rush of visitors has commenced again, and Lime Rock is one of the greatest attractions to strangers. It is estimated that over 10,000 persons called upon Miss Lewis last summer. Mr. Lewis actually counting over 9,000 of these were probably not twenty who compensated her for the trouble they gave. Her time was fully given to visitors and in consequence, she had to have her own work done. People would land on the rock, prowl over the house, quiz the family, pry into household affairs, patronizingly ask the age of each person and what they lived on and how they felt when Ida was saving souls."

Many of them were downright rude, taking photographs, newspaper clippings, and memorabilia that she had neatly tucked away and willingly shown them. Countless times she was told that they would be returned, so they were lent out, never to be seen again. Throughout her life, pranksters would mock her by pretending to need her help, yelling out "Ida, Ida, come save me," and then break into peals of laughter when she took the call seriously. Many visitors expected her to pick them up on shore and row them to her home. Others would want her to stop her chores to visit with them. Initially she complied, but ceased the practice as she got older, realizing her work would not get done.

With the onslaught of visitors came a glut of attention. She became a popular figure for painters and photographers. The new craze at the time was color postcards and many were made of her. Brewerton, her biographer, executed a fifty-by thirty-three-inch oil painting of Ida, depicting her bareheaded and rowing in an angry sea to save those hanging off a capsized boat.

Offers came in for her to see the world . . . one, as part of a traveling vaudeville act, which would have paid her $1,500. Two musical pieces were published with her name in the title, include the "Ida Lewis Mazurka," which followed a polish folk song format, and the "Ida Lewis Waltz." Multiple poems appeared. Some were published, others just penned and sent to her.

She was inundated with fan mail, as well as a few bizarre, or at least unusual, letters. She was especially touched by those who wanted to help her family. Reading that her father Hosea was stricken with paralysis following a stroke, some people sent recipes and ingredients (including oatmeal and maple syrup) for hasty pudding. Others sent money and clothing. Many letters contained requests for photos and autographs, even locks of her hair.

But by and large, the bulk of the letters came from men offering one thing: matrimony. It seemed men were mad for Ida, even if they hadn't met her. Some suitors sent photos of themselves. One fellow from West Point sent his father to meet her; he brought along his son's picture and the name of the hometown mayor as a personal character reference. He told Ida that she might learn to love his son. But Ida, taken aback, responded that the son was too young, merely an adolescent.

That same summer of 1869, Grant's vice president,

Schuyler Colfax, made a sojourn to meet the new heroine. His visit was rather extended, maybe because his own sister was a lighthouse keeper, and he felt a kindred spirit to Ida.

Harriet Colfax was the second keeper of Michigan City Light, which she took over in 1861, after her appointment was most likely arranged by her cousin, then a congressman. Formerly a schoolteacher, she moved with her brother to the city to start a newspaper and work as a typesetter for him. When her brother left town due to frail health, she stayed on and took up the position as keeper. Michigan City Light was quite different from Lime Rock. Harriet was expected to walk the long length of an elevated pier that stemmed some 1,500 feet across Lake Michigan, at the end of which was a beacon to be maintained. Rough waves and high winds lashed across the planks of wood, presenting a real danger in crossing.

Her log documented the weather, storms, and damages done to the light and pier, recounting the vicious weather of the lake and constant barrage of winter gales and blinding rainstorms. If Ida had written detailed logs like Harriet Colfax, they most likely would have been filled with short, objective entries, blandly detailing supplies and the tasks of tending the light.

Harriet's log and those of other lighthouse keepers were sparse in their detailing, but did offer a glimpse into their lives. In rare descriptions, Harriet spoke of watching the fantastic color play of the Northern Lights and the silent eclipse of the moon. She wrote about listening to the ratcheting hail off the roof of the house and pondered the beauty of a double rainbow. Unlike Ida, she had no callers of note, except for her visits from the lighthouse inspector. She was not remembered for having saved anyone with her stalwart strength. Like Ida, however, she was a small woman, and some considered her frail. She served as keeper until 1904 when she retired, and died soon after at the age of eighty.

It is likely that Colfax spoke of his cousin Harriet during his visit to Lime Rock that day. He arrived on the island uninvited and rather abruptly. He was accompanied by his new bride, General Hunt (the commander of Fort Adams), and several other officers. Ida was lying down, resting in her room, most likely trying to escape from the visitors. Colfax was greeted by her mother, who he asked to not reveal his identity to Ida. He wanted to meet her in her everyday clothes, without any special effort.

Ida came out, wiping sleep from her eyes, and was taken by surprise. Apparently the visit was cordial. At the end of their long visit, Ida walked the distinguished visitors to the docked barge, and Colfax turned to her.

He asked her if she was engaged.

Ida was indeed engaged. In fact she had been engaged for three years to a captain of a yacht from Black Rock Harbor in Bridgeport, Connecticut. While Colfax fell short of dissuading her to marry, he did say that if she did marry, she would become a Mrs. Somebody rather than Miss Ida Lewis. And more than likely, she would be forgotten. He added that she should more sensibly retain her maiden name, like many distinguished women in the public eye.

Ida's eyes flashed when she retorted. "If I should ever marry, no hope of personal gain will ever make me a party to even a conventional deceit. When I get a husband I will bear his name and no other, let the world forget me as it will."

Despite the endless stream of marriage proposals from unknown, unseen suitors, Ida chose to marry the captain whom she had met during the three summers that his yacht was docked near Lime Rock.

His name was William Heard Wilson, and he pressed Ida to marry him, particularly since her name had drawn so much public attention. His family hailed from Fairfield, Connecticut, the town next to Bridgeport. Like Ida, he was twenty-eight years old. On their marriage certificate, his occupation is listed as "seaman." Ida's is listed as "none."

A year after Colfax's visit, they married on October 23, 1870, in Newport at the Methodist Episcopalian Church on Thames Street. Ida's funeral would be held forty-one years later in that same church.

Ida's wedding was most likely a private affair and one that she would have fought to keep simple and discreet. Following her wedding to the captain, Ida made what would be the second biggest mistake of her life, following just on the heels of her first.

She left Lime Rock for the bustling harbor of Black Rock, Connecticut.

There she found a much different life than she had known in Newport. Newport Harbor had experienced its heyday in the 1700s, with the port establishing itself during the triangular trade between the West Indies and Africa. The 1800s were less prosperous, with the island never taking part in the highly profitable whaling industry that spurred the economies of much of the Eastern seaboard. Black Rock, on the other hand, rivaled much larger seaports in its level of activity. Hundreds of clippers and schooners frequented the waterways daily.

Bridgeport's shoreline, although an active vacation destination in the late 1800s, did not attract the caliber of wealthy visitors that Newport did. It was crowded, with a developed sea front. The winters were much harsher than Ida was used to, and the people were of a different cut. New Englanders in Connecticut seemed less friendly, and it was not easy to establish friendships. Ida knew no one, save her husband and new in-laws. She was not a naturally outgoing person. She quickly withered without the comfort of her surroundings and those who bolstered her spirit.

They settled in Black Rock, close to William's father, Wakeman Wilson, who owned a large plot near a point over-

looking the harbor. Even though Ida's notoriety should have
followed her, no one seemed to take much notice of her
arrival. She was more of a curiosity than anything else. Unlike
Newport, people by the hundreds didn't stop by to visit her,
and if they did, she hadn't much to show them. There was no
lantern to display, no tour to give of the white, shiny island,
no overturned boats to row out to, and no lives to save. Most
likely she didn't even have a boat to ply her skills. Ida Lewis
had nothing to do but keep house for her sometime-husband,
a seafaring yachtsman who was away more than he was home.
Perhaps as she glanced out toward the open sea outside the
harbor, she looked desperately in the direction of Lime Rock,
searching for some familiar view. Instead, she likely had the
view of another lighthouse. Fayerweather Island jutted out
into the opening of the harbor; it consisted of a skinny slip of
rocks covered with stubbly brush. On it was a tall whitewashed brick lighthouse, with an adjacent small wooden
home. In it, another woman. Another female lighthouse
keeper. The keeper of the Black Rock Light.

Kate Moore was fifty-three when Ida, then twenty-eight,
moved to Bridgeport after her 1870 marriage. It was the year
before Kate's own disabled father, for whom she faithfully
kept the wick, would finally die. Kate had cared for him,
receiving nothing in the way of recognition or recompense
from the federal government.

To keep the light of Fayerweather Island burning, Kate had
to sleep facing the tower. "I slept at home, dressed in a suit of
boy's clothes, my lighted lantern hanging at my headboard and
my face turned so that I could see shining on the wall the light
from the tower and know if anything had happened."

And if it did, it was Kate, not her father, who had to tend
it. "Our house was forty rods from the lighthouse, and to
reach it I had to walk across two planks under which on
stormy nights were four feet of water. And it was not too easy

to stay on those slippery wet boards with the whirling and the spray blinding me," Kate recounted.

Fayerweather was a skinny island that hooked into the entrance of Black Rock harbor. It could be reached only by rowboat.

Storms were quite commonplace on Fayerweather Island, as they were in Newport. But the winds were fierce enough in 1821 to completely level the lighthouse. It was rebuilt, and the light kept burning under her vigilance. Kate built her life around her time on the island. Like most lighthouse keepers, she raised animals, took care of a garden, and found other venues to make money. She tended oyster beds and carved wooden decoy ducks to sell.*

When Kate's father passed away in 1871, she took drastic measures to ensure that she would finally be compensated for her hard work of fifty-plus years. Concerned that the government might send a replacement, she holed up in the house with her father's body for a week until her own appointment came through.

Her fear was not unfounded. It was commonplace in the early years of the Lighthouse Board for keeper appointments to be made by the President or by the Secretary of the Treasury. It was common for the position to be a reward for political patronage. Often, the position went to men with no seafaring experience. All the new appointee needed to do was to show up with his slip of employment at the lighthouse and the current keeper would be expected to vacate the property immediately.

If anyone would understand Ida, it was Kate. She also was a heroine. She knew what it was like to save lives, and to haul her small rowboat out into the rolling waves in the growling face of a fierce storm. In the history of lighthouse keepers, Kate has more documented rescues attributed to her than Ida.

* They are considered collector's items today.

She saved at least twenty-three souls from the ravaging grip of the sea. She pulled half-drowned seaman from sinking wrecks in perilous storms. She risked her own life on many occasions. She had to spend countless hours with the dead bodies of sailors who had washed ashore, waiting for the government to gather them for proper burial.

But unlike Ida, Kate was ignored. Except in the twilight of her life, no newspaper reporters, society matrons, or balladeers thronged to Fayerweather to get a glimpse of the heroine there. Putting her life in harm's way was never rewarded with even a faint glimmer of limelight. She lived her isolated life, collecting $350 a year and taking care of business.

When Kate left the light, she did so without ever looking back. She retired in 1878 at eighty-four, and lived another twenty-one years to die at 105. Her life at Fayerweather was bittersweet. When asked if she missed the lighthouse life, she was matter-of-fact. "Never. The sea is a treacherous friend." Yet she lived out the rest of her life in a small house on the shore, within clear view of the lighthouse she had called home.

Unlike her, Ida desperately missed her home. She was miserable in her married life in this strange place. For without Lime Rock, without her light, she was nothing.

The marriage proved to be a disaster. So much so that she refused to speak of it, at least in public or to the media, for the remainder of her life. In published articles from later in her life, Ida had become a devout, churchgoing Christian. While she openly supported separation when a mistake had occurred, she was deeply entrenched in the belief that divorce was a sin.

"What God has joined together let no man put asunder," was the mantra she often repeated when discussing the sanctity of matrimony. Her brother Rud told reporters on the event of her death that "my sister and her husband could not live happily together. So they soon parted."

In less than two years, she left Wilson back in Bridgeport. He never once visited her for the remainder of her life, and they never divorced. She kept her legal name for a while, but eventually reverted back to her maiden name. It suited her better, and made Vice President Colfax's words prophetic.

Not much, if anything is known about Ida's marriage to Wilson. Some speculated that Wilson had a drinking problem, which was not uncommon with seafaring men of the day. Given Ida's dedication to the temperance movement, it would have been a bone of contention between the two and not easily resolved. Other reports speculated that Wilson actually died. This, however, was probably untrue, as Ida never confirmed such reports in any newspaper interviews in the years that followed their breakup. Apparently, he was alive but not in contact with her. He did not try to visit or write to her, nor she to him. At least one account told of Wilson having a depressive or manic personality, saying he was difficult to live with and prone to dark moods.

Whatever the case, given Ida's strong sense of duty and commitment to following Christian dogma, the obstacles to a life of happily-ever-after must have been substantial for her to have not stayed with him. The fact that she would never speak of the union was testimony to that.

Less than two years later, perhaps prompted by her father's death on November 17, 1872, Ida Lewis was back at her home on Lime Rock.

Chapter 5
Keeping the Wick

As the light that she kept so faithfully was a beacon to the mariner within the circle of its reach, so the light of her brave unselfish spirit became an inspiration of courage to the whole world.
—Reverend W.C. Geisler, eulogist for Ida Lewis

The life of lighthouse keepers in general could be described as arduous, mundane, and, above all, lonely. Many of the lighthouses of the nineteenth century were built in the middle of bodies of water on small islands that were constantly battered by elements such as gale-force winds. The houses and lighthouses themselves were continually damp and drafty. The smell of mildew clung to the edifices, and something was always in need of repair. Maintenance extended to all the buildings. The storms, as well as sea or lake air, set to work on the paint and wood, making it peel or rot. Enduring long periods of isolation took a stalwart person.

Compared to other lighthouse-keeping families, the Lewis family had it easier. Lime Rock was located only 220 yards from the shore (a little over twice the size of two football fields). This distance was easily spanned by a walking bridge when the lighthouse was ultimately sold in the 1920s and converted to a yacht club. Unlike other children of keepers, the younger Lewises were able to continue their education on the mainland with other children, reducing the isolation and hermitage that other keepers' families were forced to endure.

Further up the coast, Abbie Burgess, a contemporary of Ida's who moved with her family to a lighthouse when she was fourteen, had a different life with which to contend. Maine, which was sparsely populated and intensely rustic, was hardly Newport. Burgess' charge was Matinicus Rock Light, located off the roughshod coast of Maine, about midway to the New Brunswick border. The harsh brutal winters off the coast of Maine made life on the island of Lime Rock in Narragansett Harbor seem easy. In addition to the cruelty of the weather patterns and latitude lines, Matinicus Rock was stuck four miles off the south end of Matinicus Island, some twenty miles from the mainland. This lonely, desolate patch of tumbled rocks and boulders provided an excellent vantage point for ships and vessels rounding the continent and entering the treacherous shoals and ledges of the bay. The spot was home to not one, but two forty-eight-foot exposed lighthouse towers. From her youth well into her thirties, Abbie kept not one lamp, but twenty-eight.

Whether one or 1,000 lamps, keeping it trimmed, bright, and effective was an involved and detail-laden task, much harder than it appeared. Shoals, rocks, and ledges were particularly hazardous to ships and boats. Failure on the part of the light to work correctly could result in a perilous and deadly shipwreck, especially during a gale, storm, or hurricane.

Mariners and seafaring vessels depended heavily on the lights cast by these navigational aids. It's hard to imagine today, with the quantum leaps in maritime science made during the twentieth century. Mariners had to rely on much of their own innate knowledge and experience. Primary navigation was done by the night sky.

Lighthouses of the mid-nineteenth century used lamps fueled by whale oil. Depending on the time of year, the viscosity of the oil changed: thinner for summer because of the warming effects that heat had on the fuel, and thicker for the winter months for the opposite reason. If the oil was too thick, it had to be warmed to thin it out.

But the light itself was the most important aspect of any of the keeper's tasks. Its quality relied on how well the wick  was trimmed, and on clean panes of glass. For Ida, it required specific detail to the cleaning of all panes of the glass inside and out. The wick was multi-hollow and the lamp was encased in a Fresnel lens of the sixth order, which designated that the size was the smallest made since they ranged from one to six. It stood

A replica of the Lime Rock lantern.

one foot-five inches in height and 11¾ inches in diameter, which was more than suitable for the harbor.*

Fresnel lenses were invented in 1822, but it wasn't until 1840 that the first lenses were installed in U.S. lighthouses. Lime Rock, built in the 1850s, already had a Fresnel lens. The

---

* Fresnel lenses were categorized by six orders or sizes, the first being the largest at seven feet-ten inches and 72⅞ths inches, and the smallest, six, being the size of the one that hung at Lime Rock.

The room where the Lime Rock lantern was located.

circular, beveled glass lenses and prisms on the top and the bottom refracted the light, which was intensified by a magnifying glass that encased the middle of the lens. It cast the beam of light further than the lanterns that had been developed until that point. The lens was accompanied by a mechanical lamp, which burned oil that was pumped up from a reservoir below the level of the burner by means of weighted clockworks. The mechanism had to be taken care of, especially in the salt air, which tended to exact its toll on most metalwork.

In most lighthouse towers, the area at the top of the lighthouse that enclosed the lens, or "lanthorn" as it was known in Ida's time, was called the lantern room. Lime Rock's lantern room was part of the house, so Ida didn't have to leave home to tend to it. It was located on the second floor of the whitewashed stone home. The light was located in its own small room, complete with thick glass enclosure on all but the side facing the interior of the house.

Whale oil was replaced with lard in the late 1850s, due to the skyrocketing costs of the former. Smaller lights used mineral oil, and alternative fuels were experimented with, including wild cabbage, fish, olives, and finally kerosene in the 1870s. The keeper was instructed to wear a linen smock so that the more commonly worn wool would not scratch the optic or lens. Ida was required to clean the exterior of the lantern panes, clean the optic with spirits of wine (vinegar), and keep carbon and other grit from gathering on the glass. Once a year or so, it was expected the lens should be cleaned with rouge, a non-scratching substance. The keeper also had to clean the chimney of the lamp, always making sure that spare clean lamps and chimneys were on hand (usually two). The clock weight was wound and the clockworks cleaned and oiled, if needed.

All of these preparations for the coming evening were to be completed by 10:00 A.M. Then in the evening, the keeper would check the wind direction and adjust the vents to allow just enough draft into the lantern room. The entering draft would rise along the interior sides of the lantern panes, keeping them from fogging, to the top of the lantern. Wind passing horizontally through the ball vent would create a vacuum which pulled the draft up to the top of the lantern. This created a draft in the vent tube which sucked the fumes from the oil-burning lamp, up the tube, to the ball, and out of the lantern room. The vent tube was metal and directly attached to the glass chimney of the lamp.

The job didn't end when the light was lit at dusk. During the course of the evening, the keeper was required to wind the weights at least once, and trim the wicks of the lamp as necessary. She was also required to adjust the vents so that proper draft was present at all times. The chimney of the lamps had to be cleaned as well, so carbon buildup and soot didn't clog or create a backdraft.

And then there was the weather. Two decades before Lime Rock Lighthouse was completed, a fierce storm ripped through the harbor. A powerful bolt of lightening zapped Lime Rock, destroying part of the island and further scattering the rocks. Ida often talked about the winds and torrential rains, which were amplified by the open, unprotected sea. "Sometimes the spray dashes against these windows so thick I can't see out, and for days at a time the waves are so high that no boat would dare come near the rock, not even if we were starving."

In addition to maintaining the light and keeping up the home, which had to be whitewashed almost every year, Ida had to keep track of the supplies needed to do her job. This included oil, cleaning supplies, additional lamps, and a vast array of brushes that aided the keeper in her morning tasks. There was a long list of instructions that accompanied the morning cleaning after the wick was extinguished. The brushes varied in length and purpose, from feather brushes to carefully clean off the optics, to a camelhair brush to polish rouge on the prisms and silver reflectors, if there were any. Silverplate brushes cleaned the lamps and utensils, removed excess rouge, and cleaned the revolving machinery, which was made of brass and copper. These brushes were also used to apply coal tar on ironwork, a particularly disgusting task. Bottle brushes with wire-stemmed handles were used to clean the glass chimneys of the lamps and the lamp burners.

Ida and her mother kept the brushes neatly on the shelving that lined the small cubicle-shaped lantern room, along with the other supplies needed to meticulously keep the lantern dust-free and aglow.

In addition to keeping the wick trimmed and the lantern lighted, there were the numerous tasks surrounding living on an island, away from the conveniences of civilization. Many had it much worse that the Lewises, living in complete isolation because of the treacherous elements of nature.

Abbie Burgess was one of them. Like Ida, she was one of many women who maintained the light in the 1800s. Unlike Narragansett Bay, Matinicus Island jutted straight out into the Atlantic Ocean. The Lighthouse Board described the setting: "There is neither tree nor shrub, and hardly a blade of grass. The surface is rough and irregular and resembles a confused pile of loose stone. Portions of rock are frequently swept over by waves which move the huge boulders into new positions."

Abbie was also fond of writing letters. When a winter storm blew in, that mighty body of water unleashed havoc on the dwelling and surrounding animal pens. She described the scene. "Early in the day, as the tide rose, the sea made a complete breach over the rock, washing every movable thing away, and of the old dwelling not one stone was left upon another of the foundation."

The friend to whom she was writing must have once expressed a romantic wish to experience the angry ocean on the naked island, for she described, "I was back in the house with the door fastened but none too quick for at that instant my little sister, standing at the window, exclaimed, 'Oh, look! Look there! The worst sea is coming!' That wave destroyed the old dwelling and swept the Rock. I cannot think you would enjoy remaining here any great length of time for the sea is never still and when agitated, it roars, shuts out every sound, even drowning our voices."

It was through the roar of the waves that Ida had developed a keen sense of perception, to be able to hear the cries of those going down in the water just outside her island. But it was more than that. For it took strength of character and the heart of a heroine to actually go to their rescue.

Chapter 6
The Rescues Continue:
The Second, Third, and Fourth

Ever Just and Right, Angel of the Light House, Ida. In this
world there's none beside her, none more true, more brave.
In the tempest, on the wave, none more sure to save!
—Author Unknown

Jones Bridge was a small projecting wharf that stuck out
like a little finger into Newport Harbor, pointing directly
at Lime Rock. At the end of the wharf, which was a good 200
yards from the island, Ida's brother kept his skiff. It was particularly wet and cold in February 1866, with the remnants of
winter lingering and the prospect of warmer spring weather a
thought not worth entertaining. Newport's harbor settled
down in the winter, but as it was the hub of commerce and
general transportation, it still bustled with activity, inclement
weather or not. Sitting out in the harbor in the middle of

Newport Harbor added the additional element of wind to the unsavory weather mix. After almost ten years on Lime Rock, Ida and her family had been forced to get used to the temperament of the sea and adjust to the winter chill that often clung to the inside of their stone house.

And it so happened this particular night that a group of three soldiers, drunk and reeling, were making their way from the local pubs back to Fort Adams. The fort was situated on the point of a small peninsula sticking into the harbor to the west of Lime Rock. The brownish-red garrison was easy to see from the lighthouse, as it was built up on the banks of the peninsula. It was a solid structure encompassing twenty-one acres. Seeing no action during the Civil War and it being winter, life at the fort was colored by mundane activities such as maintenance and repairs.

Drinking had become a problem among the soldiers stationed there. Years before, in 1836 the Grand Jury of Rhode Island District ruled that card playing and drunkenness within the fort were breaches of law. Although "ardent spirits" were prohibited on U.S. property, shanties had been set up just outside the fort for the sale of liquor. That, plus the string of pubs in town and along the harbor, fueled the soldiers as well.

Upon seeing a moored skiff, and then eyeballing the long walk home (which was circuitous at best), the soldiers decided to borrow or steal the little boat and row their way across the large pocket of water to the garrison. It happened that the boat belonged to Ida's brother. It was indeed a more direct route, providing that they were sober enough to handle the boat and that they could swim. (Swimming would not come into fashion as a widespread sport until the early twentieth century. Most people in the mid-1850s used water for bathing and splashing, rather than competitive swimming. It was considered more a show of athletics, rather than a need or a hobby. Many of those Ida rescued might have been able to swim the hundred or so yards to the lighthouse or shore, if they had been adept swimmers.)

When the three pushed off from the wharf, they managed to get the boat into the deep water offshore, heading toward the fort. No sooner had the jolly party reached the deepest part of the harbor than one of the soldiers, trying to stand up, shoved his foot through the bottom of the boat. It quickly filled with the icy water of the February sea. Two of the men must have leapt from the sinking vessel into the frigid water and struggled to swim toward shore. Perhaps they never made it to shore, or if they did, they went AWOL, for they never appeared back at the fort, nor did they turn up for bugle call. While their bodies were searched for, they were never found, and history chooses to log their destiny as having deserted the army.

The third drunken soldier was stuck in the boat, his foot wedged. To make matters worse, the sinking boat was quickly being drawn out into the open sea by the tides. Oddly, it was within fifty or so feet of Ida's first rescue of the four capsized boys eight years earlier. Looking out on the horizon, Ida's keen eyes saw her brother's drifting boat. She dashed outside to her small rowboat that was tied to the Lime Rock dock, and seized the oars.

Within minutes she maneuvered the skiff to the wreck, working herself around to its stern. She reached overboard to hook the inebriated, semi-conscious man by the arm onto the boat, hoping to drag him to the island. But she was forced to pull his unresponsive body slowly into the skiff. Using all of her strength and persistence, she tugged at the soaked, frozen man—as he wailed drunkenly for help—and was able to topple him into the back end of the boat, loosening his foot from the sinking wreck.

During that second rescue, Ida wrenched her back as the man's dead weight and stupor almost caused him to pull her into the depths with him. Exhausted and in pain, Ida managed to get into the back end of her skiff, and rowed him back to her home at the lighthouse, where he was well-fed and given a change of clothes. In reminiscing about the incident, she recalled that her physical injury took more than a year to heal and she never heard from the soldier again. To make matters worse, she said, "He never returned the clothing."

This was to be the scenario for most of Ida's rescuees. She had to wait until her fifth rescue to receive any appreciation or notoriety. The young soldier was hardly grateful. At the time of the rescue, she was barely the same age at which acclaim was heaped upon Grace Darling, the woman with whom Ida would be forever linked.

As was Ida's custom, she never spoke of the heroic rescue. She would remain obscure and unknown, among the ranks of so many other female lighthouse keepers of her time, who went about their grueling lives in relative anonymity.

It was less than a year later, on another cold wintry morning in January 1867, that Ida's rescue skills were once again tested.

August Belmont was one of the elite of Newport. Belmont was a banker who owned an elaborate estate in town. He also owned sheep. And like many of his class, he had hired Irish farmhands to help maintain his fields.

Immigration to Newport was fueled by the shipbuilding industry. The Irish had come to work in the shipyards, and were solicited to help build the fort and work on the farms. They eventually made up a significant population in what is now Newport's fifth district.

A southeast gale was blowing that January morning at around nine or ten. And three Irish farmhands were moving a valuable, prize-winning sheep for Belmont through the town's Main Street, when it suddenly broke away from them and trotted toward the shore. The three followed and tried to corral the animal, but it plunged directly into the harbor, right off Jones Wharf. Desperate, the three watched their charge drifting slowly out toward Lime Rock.

On shore, they raced alongside the moving, bleating animal. Ida's brother had purchased a new skiff, which he kept tied up on the wharf, the former being lost in the previous year's rescue of the drunken soldier. Spotting the boat, they leapt into it. Hardly seafaring men, the three tried desperately to paddle after the drifting sheep in the middle of the blustering winds, fighting the cresting waves that tossed the boat about.

Inexperienced in how to row a boat, the men knew they were in trouble. The waves came crashing over the edge, and the skiff began to take on water. The three men began to panic, and started to shout for help. The vessel capsized, and all three fought to cling to its hull. Ida had been sewing in the kitchen near a window when she heard the frantic yells over the howling wind. She saw her brother's boat topple sideways, and all three men go under a wave.

Ida wasted no time in getting into her rescue craft. She dipped the oars expertly into the choppy waves, and dipped her chin into her chest as she moved through the water toward the screaming men, whose numb hands were losing their grip on the slippery hull. Ida recalled their cries, laced with Gaelic dialect. As she got closer, she could hear their Irish brogue as they prayed out loud to the deities and begged for their lives. "Oh Holy Virgin, and be Jabbers, have you come to save me?" one man called to her with a terrified look. The wind whipped around her and rain bit into her hands as she helped them into the skiff. Shivering and gushing appreciation, they begged to be dropped off back on shore, hoping to recapture their charge. Once she had landed them back on solid ground, they pleaded with her to rescue the runaway sheep. Fearful of the wrath of their boss, they were near hysteria.

Ida relented. She shoved away from the shore and headed back into the battling waves toward the struggling sheep, who was fighting weakly against the currents that were moving it toward open sea. Ida dug her oars in deeper and moved the skiff up beside the sinking animal. With great difficulty, she braced her footing against the slippery sides of the boat. With her hand lassoed around a length of rope, she bent into the waves to hook the loop around the beast's neck. The sheep, swallowing water and afraid, would not comply.

Ida regrouped several times, struggling to keep herself anchored in the rowboat, while keeping her back to the fierce wind and rain. Finally, she was able to secure the rope around the frenzied animal's neck, and with a wrench on the rope secured it to the side of the boat. Trying to pull the animal over the stern into the boat would have been too much, even for Ida Lewis. She rowed the boat, sheep in tow, into shore. The farmhands wept with appreciation. But the appreciation ended there. Ida never heard from the farmhands again, nor did she hear from August Belmont. There was never any compensation made to her for saving his prize sheep's life.

Her fourth rescue was not far behind. Just two weeks after Ida returned Belmont's prize sheep and his farmhands, she was called to duty again. The underwater terrain between Lime Rock and the town had several rock masses, which would become exposed during the ebbing tides. One of these sunken rocks was marked with a spindle, or stick, which jutted from just under the water's brim. It was meant to warn sailors and pleasure craft of its whereabouts.

But it was midnight. Maybe the boatman did not see the spindle in the darkness, even with the light from the nearby beam. Perhaps he just plain ignored it, being unfamiliar with the area and not realizing that its purpose was to ward him away from danger. As he was sailing into the harbor, his sailboat struck the rock head on. Aided by the tide that was starting to come into the harbor, the boat wedged itself on the jagged tip of the rock. A winter Nor'easter was moving in and gaining strength. The cold water flowed around the sailor, who began to scream for help. His cries were drowned out by the wind and icy rain that rushed around him. His entreaties were lost in the expanse of water that ended where the crush of waves smacked against the shore of the small lighthouse island.

As the hours ticked by toward dawn, it was all the sailor could do to hang on. He struggled not to be washed away as he clung to the rigging, frozen saltwater stiffening his joints and locking them into position around the mast. The tide had crept in through the darkness of the night. The light from Lime Rock cast a safe glow in the distance as Ida and her family slept. With the rising water line and bitingly cold waves, he tried to inch up higher, certain that death was upon him.

As dawn neared, the gray sky brightened, but the rains continued. Around six that morning, Ida's mother rose to check the lantern. She moved to the kitchen to light the fire in the hearth, and upon her cursory glance out of the kitchen window, she saw the very top of the mast of the submerged boat. A closer look revealed the head of a man. The water had risen to just under his chin, and he was gulping for air as waves crashed over his head, forcing him to hold his breath. With a scream, she roused her daughter, who quickly put on her clothes, and slipped into the rowboat at the base of the island.

He must have heard her call in the dawn air, as she yelled to him to hold on. She was on the way. Within minutes, her swift oar strokes brought her skiff to the sunken rock and the sailor, who was minutes away from becoming completely submerged under the tide. Ida hauled his frigid, water-logged body into the stern of the skiff. Hypothermia had set in, and when he hit the bottom of the boat, he was completely unconscious. Without panic, Ida worked to revive him. He slowly came to, sputtering up sea water and working his arms spastically to bring back feeling. Satisfied that he was conscious, she angled her oars toward the warmth of her home.

But he begged her to reverse direction, and to take him to the wharf on shore. She tried to convince him otherwise, and pressed him to allow her family to feed him breakfast and give him a change of clothing. But he was unrelenting and she gave into his request, assuming he might not be right in the head. She deposited him on *terra firma*. She never heard from the man again. His name was never known.

Some weeks later, Ida received a note from the owner of the wrecked sailboat. Instead of a thank you, the polite missive stated that he gladly would have given Ida $50 if she had let the man drown. Apparently he had stolen the boat.

Chapter 7
Losing Heart

Not in the clamor of the crowded street
Not in the shouts and plaudits of the throng
But in ourselves, our triumph and defeat.
—Henry Wadsworth Longfellow

The years were beginning to weigh heavily on Ida. She had, in essence, been the lighthouse keeper of Lime Rock since her father's stroke. Even with her mother's assistance, she bore the brunt of the responsibility for her family. Her primary focus, however, was the light. The lantern had to be meticulously maintained as well as kept lit. While her mother had toiled in the early years to keep the light, she had other worries. Ida's sister Hattie, who was never healthy as a child, had grown into frail adulthood. Her lungs were weak and partial to infection, and Zoradia, herself crippled by chronic pain in the joints and easily fatigued, had to tend to her continually and leave most of everything else on Ida's shoulders.

Ida's failed marriage found her back at Lime Rock less than two years after the wedding. She was elated to return to the peace and contentment she found on her island home. But with her arrival came the sinking realization that she would take her place as titular head of the household. While she had longed to be reunited with the lantern and the fine tasks of keeping it nightly, she realized that she faced nothing more than a life of manual servitude.

Her father had passed away in 1872, after years of being an invalid. At the end of his life, he had to have his food cut and fed to him. His passing came almost as a relief to the family. Zoradia took over as keeper after his death. As was the custom, she assumed the position in name so as to continue receiving a salary. But it was Ida who continued to keep the light. Her mother was no doubt wholly relieved to have capable, stalwart Ida back at home. It was, however, beginning to bother Ida that after years of being the keeper of the light, and being referred to as such in newspaper clippings and the like, she still was not appointed.

Her father had been crippled only four months after moving to Lime Rock in 1858. At that time, her mother was more helpful and did most of the tending to the light. She should have been appointed in her husband's stead. But it wasn't until his death in 1872 that her mother appears as keeper, with no official appointment. Her mother wasn't the keeper, Ida was, and had been for a long time. Would she have to wait until the unfortunate death of her mother until finally receiving her rightful recognition?

The years were passing slowly, marked mainly by routine. With each passing summer came the onslaught of curiosity seekers whom, even though Ida was used to them, she never welcomed. She treated the visitors as part of her job, and dutifully gave tours and answered questions. Gifts continue to pour in, and Ida was appreciative of them all. The local newspapers seemed to keep a running tally, reporting on strange requests and gifts that were out of the ordinary. In 1870, months before her wedding, she received a pair of lace white stockings from the Chicago White Sox. The *Boston Journal* called the $500 gift, which had the emblem of the "great American game" embroidered upon them in spun-gold, a "perfectly useless gift."

"Like the majority of her presents . . . a box of good English hose would have been more acceptable. Presents keep pouring in, flowers, dogs, silver, flags, etc., of no use to her. The salary of a harbor lighthouse keeper is not too much . . . The silk flag framed on her wall is a nice thing to look at and the medals are very pretty to handle. The sewing machine she could not get time to use, and the beautiful boat has lain idle from want of strength to use the oars. Of cash she had very little and flowers and canary birds were not of much value."

Ida was fast becoming fodder for celebrity-style gossip in the papers, which led to some outlandish reports about her life. One report stated that contrary to popular belief, Ida could not swim. Another stated that she had left the lighthouse to work in a restaurant.

But regardless of whether or not she had the official appointment, she continued her vigilance over the waters, and on numerous occasions set her skiff out on the billowy sea to aid mariners and others in trouble. Not all of Ida's rescues were documented. Lack of eyewitnesses and Ida's own modesty kept them from getting the attention they deserved. Never one to herald her own cause or tout her own rescues— they were always brought to the public fore by someone else—many of her selfless acts of bravery were never recorded. It is difficult to know how many actual lives were saved, but even the briefs in the local papers point to a substantial number more than the documented eighteen.

During the 1870s, Ida's life developed into a routine—one centered around her beloved lantern. But growing slowly inside her was a deep resentment. The government never once considered officially appointing her lighthouse keeper. Her mother had assumed the job, as did so many other women, taking over the position handily, but with no formal recognition from the government. The reason for this was mainly financial. There was no pension in place for appointed lighthouse keepers, who were always men. When they passed away or were disabled, their wives, daughters, or spinster sisters would take over the position, and continue to receive the annual salary. Unlike their male counterparts, these women's appointments never had to go through the official appointment process.

The first female lighthouse keeper that history remembers is Hannah Thomas, who lived with her husband at Plymouth harbor in the late 1700s. When her husband was called to military duty to fight the British in the American Revolution, Hannah was left to tend to the lights alone. Most lighthouses had gardens and animals to help offset food costs. Oftentimes, male lighthouse keepers also ran other businesses off the island, such as fishing, oystering, or clamming. In order to keep the income coming in from these side businesses, the wives had to tend the lights for weeks at a time, while their husbands traveled to the nearest shore town to do business or sell their harvests.

Repairs had to be made and records kept, as well as supplies ordered. All of this fell on the wife or family, especially if the keeper was ill or aging. If she didn't choose to stay on, she would maintain the light until her husband's replacement arrived. By the mid-1800s it was becoming more and more of a practice to have female keepers, so it is no surprise that by the early twentieth century, some two hundred-eleven women had been appointed lighthouse keepers, and twice that number were assistant keepers, oftentimes daughters or wives.

But this wasn't enough for Ida. She was not the keeper, her mother was. And when her mother died, the appointment would most likely be passed on to her. But it did not come as an official recommendation with the same meaning as if she had been a man, appointed in her own right.

This had become increasingly important to Ida, and for reasons lost to time, the whole matter began to wear on her. Perhaps her celebrity status, which was no longer at a fever pitch but did manage to keep her in the local papers, was actually a double-edged sword. Although she never asked for recognition, the fact that it landed with both feet on her doorstep made her think more seriously about her acts of bravery. It was not as if fame went to her head, but she continued to be celebrated as the most famous lighthouse keeper in the world, easily surpassing England's Grace Darling. It had to have at least led her to wonder why no recognition came to her from the government.

By all accounts, Ida was a modest and retiring person, often shrugging off her acts of unsurpassed bravery as if they were nothing. After all, life-saving was considered part of the job. The Lighthouse Service rarely published details and barely mentioned rescues in its annual reports. "During the fiscal year, services in saving of life and property were rendered and acts of heroism performed by employees of the Lighthouse Service on vessels or at stations on ___ occasions," with the total being filled out for that given year.

There was something more, however. For beneath the stoic disregard of her feats, Ida had come to believe in the person whom the media and society had created. This is not to say that she was an arrogant person or suffered from an inflated ego. It was only human to get somewhat swept away in the face of the publicity and public adoration showered upon her in the course of less than five years. She felt she was more than deserving of the appointment that continued to elude her.

Perhaps it was even something more basic. Although claiming to share no interest or opinion about the women's rights movement, perhaps she was beginning to feel firsthand the sting of being passed over, ignored, or merely patted on the head for a job well done. In her own mind, Ida had to know that the courage she demonstrated during her numerous rescues was uncommon, even for a man. Though she may have drawn no distinction in her mind of the difference between men and women when it came to life's tasks, perhaps it began to dawn on her that the rest of the world did. Being treated as the eldest son by her father may have been where her sense of equality began. It was expected that she do all the tasks that a boy, and then a man, would. When did the roles change?

"Anyone who thinks it is un-feminine to save lives has the brains of a donkey," she said. Ida had been compared to a man in many instances and by many writers. An article in *Ladies Home Journal* was one of many that drew this analogy. "It is almost everyone's first surprised comment, spoken or not, expecting to see a female Hercules. Her eyes are a clear, honest blue gray, her face rather severe in repose, brightens in speech, and shows where a few unusual dimples lurk. Her firm, square jaw is an index of the strength of will that has made it possible for her to brave peril that many a strong man would decline. Fate does not often throw in one person's path, to be sure, so many opportunities to distinguish oneself for heroism, but it is not everyone who would have accepted them all so promptly."

And accept it she did, time and again.

It was November 1877 when Ida's bravery was once against tested on the waters of Newport Harbor. It involved soldiers who were musicians in the band at Fort Adams. Winter and alcohol seemed to bring out the worst in them, and once again, a groggy group of three decided to take a boat home, rather than travel by foot. No sooner had they gotten the skiff into deep water than it capsized.

Not much is known of this rescue, except that Ida was quick to land in her boat and drop her oars in the white peaks of the sea. She did this with such ferocity that she made it to the wreck in record speed. However, hauling the soggy load in combination with the incoming winter snow proved to be exhausting. The load was so heavy after she got aboard the skiff that she had to stop several times on the perilous journey back to the house to recover her strength.

The rescue proved to be too much for Ida. She became very sick with what is suspected to be diphtheria, a bacterial infection in the throat that causes a thick membranous substance, making it difficult to breathe and swallow. The strain of the rescue compounded with exposure to the icy seas and winds left her with a high fever and general weakness. Month after month, Ida lay still, using her energy only to clean the lantern and perform some light housework.

For the first time, the newspapers pondered in print about her future. Ida still had not been officially appointed lighthouse keeper and she was making no money of her own. There was talk of a pension for the first time, something to help her subsist in her old age, when she was no longer able to rescue drunken soldiers, wayward lads, or runaway sheep. The fact that the government, despite all the attention this modern-day heroine had garnered, did nothing to officially recognize her was demoralizing.

The lack of an appointment took on insult proportions.

✢ ✢ ✢

By the middle of 1878, Ida had finally recovered from her long sickness. On April 18th of that year, the family rowed to the mainland to celebrate brother Hosea's (Hosey's) marriage to twenty-three-year-old Ellen Moran. She was an Irish

Catholic girl who had been born in England. As was the custom of the time, the religion of the wife was respected, so the wedding was at St. Mary's Catholic Church. Hosea was twenty-eight and a teamster, having turned his back on pursuing a life on the water like his father and sister. Plagued with ill-health and weak lungs like his sister Hattie, living on the water was not the best place for him. Hosea and his bride moved to a small house in downtown Newport.

The next year, Ida felt the diphtheria coming on again. The newspaper lauded her quick thinking as it reported, she "remembered that kerosene was an unfailing remedy." Having gallons of it on hand to fuel the lantern, she swallowed an entire tablespoon, which of course forced her to vomit violently. Then she saturated a cloth in the noxious fuel and wrapped it around her throat. She continued to do this several more times, until she felt she had killed the diphtheria, and fell into an exhausted sleep.

She warded off the illness.

Throughout the 1870s, whether she realized it or not, Ida had met and subsequently made some very powerful acquaintances, acquaintances that would serve her well.

Ida had never actually met General Ambrose Everett Burnside, the Civil War general known for making sideburns popular. Burnside served as governor of Rhode Island after the war, and in 1874 was elected to the U.S. Senate. Word of Ida's rescue the year before in 1877 caught his ear, as did her lack of appointment to the position. Sometime in 1878, he decided to pick up the mantle for Ida, and inquired among the powers that be why Ida Lewis, famed heroine of Lime Rock, was still not appointed as lighthouse keeper. No one could answer his question.

Outraged at the slight to this brave woman who had been faithfully discharging her duties without pay or title, the military general started making noise.

As the *New York Times* would later report, "She would not
have gotten the position had it not have been for the rescue of
three intoxicated musicians who were just disappearing under
the waves . . . . The famous general's sense of justice was revolted
and he didn't rest until he had obtained the title as well as the
duties of the office. It was almost the last act of his life."

On January 21st of the next year, 1879, Ida finally
received the appointment for which she had been so long
waiting. It had been arranged at the hands of Burnside, and
ushered along by her political connections in the U.S. Navy
and Lighthouse Bureau. Signed by then-Secretary of the Treasury John Sherman, the official letter read:

> *You are hereby appointed Keeper of the Lighthouse at
> Lime Rock, R.I., at a salary of $750 per annum, vice
> Mrs. Zoradia Lewis resigned. This appointment is
> conferred upon you as a mark of my appreciation for
> your noble and heroic efforts in saving human lives.*

Ida had almost given up all hope. She must have heard
early on in 1878 of the appointment going through, for she
sent a note off to Burnside with the pending news in the early
summer, to which he responded on July 1, 1878. In his own
handwriting on a small U.S. Senate postcard, rimmed with
the black border of mourning (indicating the recent death of
his wife), he wrote:

> *My dear Mrs. Wilson—I thank you for your kind
> letter of the 30th last. It gave me great pleasure to be
> of service to you, particularly as you so well deserve all
> that the government has done for you. I wish it could
> do more. With wishes for your health and happiness,
> I remain very truly yours, AE Burnside.*
> *If you will kindly send the letter from the Light-*

*house Board to me. I will take copy of it and return
the original to you.*

The appointment came just before what many consider
to be the most perilous rescue of Ida's life and one that would
garner her a second wave of worldwide recognition and
renewed fame. Ida was finally and officially the keeper of
Lime Rock.

✦ ✦ ✦

Deep winter was always an unpleasant time on Lime Rock.
Gale-force winds off the Atlantic Ocean were often accompanied by roiling black waves and the raw, bone-biting temperatures that only wet winter can bring. To make matters worse,
it was common during the latter months of winter in the late
nineteenth century for massive chunks of frozen ice to drift
into the harbor, isolating the small lighthouse island in its
own frozen tundra. The repeating cycle of daytime sun and
overnight freezing fused the small ice patches into a larger ice
mass which often extended from the mainland out into the
harbor. The frozen outstretch was so common by February,
locals knew where the safe spots ended and the thinner, more
treacherous ice began.

Overall, the soldiers comprised a significant portion of
Newport's population. Those stationed there, like the rest of
islanders, knew about the frozen patches of ice that melded
together to create seemingly safe ice passages. They also knew
the risk involved in treading beyond the few hundred feet of
so-called "safe ice" that paralleled the shore. Beyond that
point the ice became somewhat thin and mushy, with spotty
holes where the drift ice had not fully closed in.

But at five o'clock in the afternoon on February 4, 1881,
what two of the soldiers at Fort Adams knew had no bearing

An illustration from Harper's Weekly, *showing Ida (center) with her mother and disabled father.*

on what they eventually did. They set out on foot from
town—where they had apparently been patronizing several
grog houses—and headed toward the fort. Giuseppe Gianetti
and Freddie Tucker were both privates stationed at the fort.
Hoping to cut some time off their journey, they ventured
onto the ice in the harbor, making their way past Lime Rock.
They were drunk to the point where they either misjudged
where the safe ice ended and patchy ice began, or to the point
where they just didn't care.

Ida and her family were in the kitchen of their small home
on Lime Rock preparing dinner. Whether it was dinnertime
or not, the kitchen was the preferred place to be, as the bitter
chill easily penetrated the stone structure of the lighthouse.
The small fireplace in the kitchen provided the most warmth
in the home.

As the soldiers tromped over the crunchy ice into Bretton
Cove, where the ice was notoriously thin, Ida and her mother
caught sight of them from the window. In that instance, a
loud, terrifying cracking noise pierced through the air as the

ice gave way under their weight. They slid into the murky, freezing depths below, disappearing from view. Their eerie screams pierced the twilight.

Ida's mother fainted, while Hattie rushed to tend to her. Without a second thought to grab a coat or outer gear, Ida raced to the door, grabbing a clothesline instead. Hattie yelled to her brother Rudolph for help, who was in another part of the house. He followed after Ida a few minutes later.

Out on the ice, Ida raced toward the men, who were crying out in pain as the freezing Atlantic Ocean numbed their limbs. Wary of the condition of the precarious makeshift floor beneath her feet, she moved toward the floundering men gingerly, trying the ice with her shoe points. Once within striking distance, she tossed the clothesline to two sets of grasping hands.

It missed.

She reeled in the slack and tried again. Yelling for only one of them to grab hold at a time, they obviously misunderstood her. Both soldiers grabbed the line. Ida drew in the slack, and began to tug and pull the rope backwards, using her slight weight and strong determination against their two bodies. She again yelled for them to let go. They began to panic, and Ida cinched the rope tighter. She moved even closer to the treacherous thin ice. She began to pull backwards with all the strength in her arms and upper back, begging the men to release the cord.

They instead yanked forward on the clothesline. With a startling jerk, Ida plunged forward and stumbled onto the mushy ice, which easily gave way under her weight. Her skirts quickly filled like a balloon as her body was pulled into the harbor's icy depths. Her bustle, representative of the Victorian style of the time, further weighted Ida down. The air rushed out of her lungs as the shock of the frigid water hit her, and the steel fittings of her corset sent stabbing pains through her chest. She felt herself being pulled under by the weight of the struggling, sinking soldiers.

As was her hallmark, Ida managed to keep her wits about her. She slackened the clothesline. A capable swimmer—in fact, she was touted the best swimmer in Newport by the age of fourteen—Ida drew upon her skill to force her numb limbs into action. She moved her soaking body back to the edge of broken-away ice, never losing grip on the icy clothesline, and hauled herself up, edging forward until the ice could hold her weight.

Her sickly sister Hattie watched in horror from the kitchen window, ineffectively nursing their mother back to consciousness. Ida was soaked to the skin, with more than ten yards of wet skirts clinging to her in below-freezing temperatures, trying to brace her slim body against the dead weight of the drunken soldiers. Finally, one of the soldiers relinquished his hold on the rope, allowing Ida a window of opportunity to move the other onto the ice shore.

Propelled to action, she lost no time once afoot, and caught up the slack on the clothesline, to which now one sinking soldier still clung. With her concentrated might, she pulled the man toward her. With one final heave, his torso slid onto the stronger ice, and she managed to drag him onto solid footing.

At this point, her brother Rudolph arrived and together they used the clothesline and their combined strength to pull the second soldier, now almost unconscious, out of the harbor. They brought the men back to the house to change clothes and warm themselves, and then they were transported to Newport Hospital for several days before being discharged.

Soon after that, the newspapers latched onto Ida's latest act of bravery. Published accounts appeared throughout the country of how this slight woman, braced with unshakeable courage, risked her own life to rescue the two soldiers. Recountings of the incident omitted mention of her brother.

A letter arrived shortly after the lifesaving, dated February 11, 1881. In thin, precise script on a small sheet of lined paper, a heartfelt note was penned by one of the soldier's mothers.

> *Dear good brave woman. What can I say. What can I do for I cannot thank you half enough on paper for saving the life of my Dear Boy, Freddie O. Tucker. Only last Sunday, I was reading of your bravery in rescuing two men. I little thought one of them was my dear boy. I have always felt an* (sic) *desire to see you and if nothing happens then I will visit Newport this summer then I will see you. But if you are sick, you send for me. I will come and do for you. This is one of my wishes, I wish I was rich.*

The second page of the letter is lost to time. It will never be known if Ida actually received her at the lighthouse, or if she even responded to the letter. But it is one of the only surviving letters of gratitude that Ida received.

Ida spoke about the incident. "I was pretty strong then. It was hard work pulling those men out to strong ice, and it made my arms lame." About the source of her uncommon strength in the throes of that event, she said, "I don't know. I ain't particularly strong. The Lord Almighty gives it to me when I need it. That's all."

Despite her humility and deference to God, this single act of bravery would hardly go unnoticed. U.S. Customs Collector Cozzens, upon hearing about the dangerous rescue, contacted the Lighthouse Board.

Ida caught her first wind that something amazing was going to happen to her when she received correspondence from Rear Admiral of the U.S. Navy John Rodgers on February 11, 1881, just days after the rescue. In it he told Ida that

Congress by Act of 1874 had passed legislation providing a medal for "recognition of such services to humanity and prescribed the evidence upon which it should be awarded." She was being nominated for the recognition. In the process, the Inspector would have to obtain and forward affidavits about the rescue, which would then be reviewed by the Secretary of the Treasury.

Eyewitness accounts of that day were taken from everyone involved, including her mother, Hattie, the two soldiers saved, and the commanding officer at the fort. They all concurred that Ida's rescue put her life in great peril and at risk of serious injury. As a result, Ida was honored with a gold Life Saving Medal of the First Class for her heroism.

The following September, the medal was transmitted to her, and with it a formal letter from Secretary of the Treasury William Windom, who wrote:

> *These deeds have already won for you national distinction, and it is peculiarly appropriate that you should receive the national lifesaving medal in commemoration of your brave acts as a life saver, while it is an occasion for added satisfaction that such a memorial of unquestionable heroism should have been won by a woman.*

At noon on October 11, 1881, the official presentation was made, with both Collector Cozzens and former Collector Macy present, as well as the mayor and other city dignitaries. Ida Lewis was accompanied by her sister, Hattie.

As Ida sat and listened to the presentation, her hands were neatly folded in front of her and on her dress she wore her Sorosis Society gold pin, neatly clipped at her throat. Doing the honor was F. E. Chadwick, who was then a lieutenant with the U.S. Navy and who had turned out to be, along with his wife, a guardian angel for Ida.

> *It is my pleasant duty to be the bearer to Mrs. Lewis of the highest token of merit of its kind which can be given in this country, the Life Saving Medal of the first class to be conferred by the United States Government for in the words of the law itself, extreme heroic daring, involving imminent personal danger on the part of the rescuer . . . I would preface this by here recording the great modesty which Mrs. Lewis has shown in relation to her noteworthy acts: she has kept no personal records of what she has done: has preserved none of the many laudatory newspaper notices which have frequently appeared regarding her, knew scarcely any of the dates of her actions, and in most instances did not know the names even of the men she had saved. This very unusual disregard of the causes of her distinction was brought to light in the investigations necessary to make an authentic report of her many rescues to the Lighthouse Board.*

With that, he launched into an accounting of the rescues, as best could be remembered and accounted for.

In the 1881 Annual Report of U.S. Life Saving Service, Ida Lewis' write-up was extensive, but culminated in praise of her courage.

"The action on her part showed unquestionable nerve, presence of mind, and dashing courage . . . All witnesses unite in saying the rescue was accomplished at the imminent risk of the rescuer's life."

It was the first time since Congress passed the act in 1874 awarding these medals to civilians that a woman received the honor, which is reserved for exceptional bravery in rescuing lives. The act also won her the gold medal from the Humane

Society of the Commonwealth of Massachusetts, which had never previously awarded honors to anyone outside of the state. Ida was the exception.

This was her second-to-last documented rescue, the documentation coming from a report compiled by the inspector himself in the process of obtaining the affidavits. Relying on memory, it was Zoradia and Ida who were predominately interviewed as to how many rescues Ida actually performed to date. Recalling as many as she could, and relying in part on Brewerton's account, Ida came up with what would be considered the official total at the end of her life: eighteen.

By this time, Ida was thirty-nine years old and had been the official lighthouse keeper for three years. She was also presented with a purse of gold coins and a silver teapot (which cost $150 at the time), in honor of the rescue. These gifts came from the soldiers and officers at Fort Adams. The teapot was her most valued trophy. She often showed it off to visitors and kept it prominently displayed in her home. With exception of the teapot and the silk flag presented to her by Jim Fisk on Independence Day 1868, Ida never displayed gifts. Rather, she kept them meticulously in a keepsake basket, contained in the original trappings in which they were given to her, the hinges on the cases rusting in the sea air. While they must have held some significance for her, she never was to take advantage of the entitlement that each one gave to her. That entitlement, along with the medals, also remained neatly tucked away.

An artist's rendition of Newport Harbor in the late 1800s.
Note Lime Rock Lighthouse at the right.

Chapter 8
A Solitary Life (1881–1911)

I love it. I could not be contented elsewhere.
—Ida Lewis, referring to life on Lime Rock

Newport had long been attracting the wealthy to its scenic shores, earning its reputation as a playground for the rich and famous. Many of the predecessors to the opulent mansions that dot the island's north shore were already inhabited by the country's wealthiest, drawn to Newport in the late 1800s. This was the era of the Industrial Revolution.

The country was between two great wars—the Civil War and World War I. And it was literally a coming of age for the United States, for in a period of less than fifty years, it transformed itself from a rural republic into an urban state. The frontier had vanished and it its place, great factories and steel mills, transcontinental railroad lines, flourishing cities, and vast agricultural holdings marked the land. And with them came monopolies, poor factory working conditions, slums, and a growing disparity between the very wealthy and the very poor.

The twenty or thirty years preceding the Civil War laid the groundwork for the end of the century. And the war stimulated manufacturing and speeded up an economic process—whose fundamental factors were the exploitation of iron, steam, and electrical power—as well as the forward march of science and invention. The 36,000 patents granted before 1860 were but a drop in the bucket compared to the flood of inventions to follow. From 1860 to 1890, 440,000 patents were issued, and in the first quarter of the twentieth century, the number reached nearly a million.

During that time frame, the world watched Thomas Edison make practical use of electricity (1880); Samuel F. B. Morse perfect electrical telegraphy (1844), linking distant parts of the continent with a network of poles and wires; and Alexander Graham Bell exhibit a telephone instrument (1876). In addition, the tempo of business was quickened by the invention of the typewriter in 1867, the adding machine in 1888, and the cash register in 1897. The linotype composing machine, the rotary press, and paper-folding machinery made it possible to print 240,000 eight-page newspapers in an hour. The boon of invention and growth of big business and monopolies resulted in a new level of productivity in virtually all fields. And many of the major players chose very handsome trappings for themselves.

Elsie French Vanderbilt was one of them. A vibrant, schooled woman, she had what many considered the great fortune to marry Alfred Gwynne Vanderbilt, great grandson of Commodore Vanderbilt and son of Alice and Cornelius Vanderbilt. Born Ellen French Tuck in 1881, Elsie, as she was known, was the daughter of the president of the Manhattan Trust Company. The marriage occurred in the same year that Ida received the great honor of being singled out as the first woman to be awarded the gold U.S. Life Saving Medal. In addition, Ida was the first woman and first non-resident to receive the prestigious silver medal from the Humane Society of the Commonwealth of Massachusetts.

The society papers described Elsie as "tall and divinely fair with a wealth of titian-coloured hair and brilliant complexion, made more beautiful by surf and sun." She spent much of her childhood growing up at Harbourview, an exquisite estate built by her parents on the shore of Newport, looking out at Lime Rock Light. Unlike the Vanderbilt family that she was to marry into, Elsie lived most of the time in Newport, rather than just the summers. Ida Lewis was already a legend during her childhood, and Elsie would look across the still waters of the harbor, wondering about the woman whom she could only see as a small spot on the island.

Newport's proximity to New York City, access to the ocean, bustling port, and attractive sweeps of landscape were a natural lure to the wealthy. The massive fortunes garnered during this period helped usher in the Gilded Age, which was punctuated by blatant political corruption in the 1870s. The period took its name from an 1873 novel by Mark Twain in collaboration with Charles Dudley Warner, an essayist, humorist, and editor for *Harper's Magazine.* Considered to be a jab at the excesses of the time, the novel provided strong commentary on the political and social climate of the times.

Summer homes were common among the well-to-do, as was traveling abroad and fine-tuning social graces. The preoccupation, however, of these early vacationers with building monstrous homes in the grand style of European castles had just begun to manifest itself in the late 1800s.

Beechwood Mansion was built earlier in 1851 by a New York City merchant named Daniel Parrish. It would become the future home of William Backhouse Astor Jr., grandson of John Jacob Astor, the German immigrant who made himself

the richest man in America by investing in fur trading and
real estate. Astor bought it in 1881 and poured $2 million
into its renovation. It was William B. who married the infa-
mous Caroline Schermerhorn, who insisted on being called
"The Mrs. Astor," the undisputed Queen of American Society.
A social snob of the utmost degree, it was she who devised the
"famous 400"—a list of 213 families and individuals whose
lineage could be traced back at least three generations. The list
is better known as the social registry, or blue book. Her son,
John Jacob Astor IV, would go down in history as the wealthiest man to die on the *Titanic*.

But for the eight weeks of summer that Mrs. Astor actually resided in the multi-million dollar Beechwood mansion,
she presided over the elite social activities that only the privileged could enjoy. The highlight of the summer was Mrs.
Astor's Summer Ball; being invited to the event was the ultimate proof of one's social worth. It was the Astors who
brought New York high society to Newport.

Keeping up with the Astors was no easy task, but the Vanderbilts had the power and means to do so. In the late 1800s,
an extensive wooden summer "cottage" perched on a cliff
overlooking the ocean was purchased by Cornelius Vanderbilt
II, grandson of steamship and railroad tycoon Commodore
Vanderbilt and chairman of the New York Central Railroad.
Following a fire, Cornelius tore down the rest of the home
and replaced it in 1893 with what is the grandest of all the
Newport mansions, The Breakers. The seventy-room Renais-
sance-style palazzo was inspired by sixteenth-century palaces
of Genoa and Turin, and is built predominately of international marble.

Perhaps he was influenced by his younger brother William
and his bride Alva, who also decided to vacation in Newport
in 1888. They chose to build a mansion from scratch rather
than purchase one of the existing wooden-frame, oversized

"cottages." They commissioned a fantastic mansion, made completely of marble, to replicate the Petit Trainon in Versailles. The Marble House was finished in 1893, and marked the transformation of Newport from a quiet summer colony of wooden houses to a legendary resort community of stone homes. Though it was quaintly called a "cottage," the $11-million (by contemporary cost accounts) mansion was the first of the "Gilded Age" homes to be completed. The 500,000 square feet of marble was said to cost $7 million of the total cost.

The Vanderbilt boys, the Astors, and a host of other captains of industry like Edward Julius Berwind—millionaire coal merchant and owner of another mansion, The Elms—had put Newport on the social register. The twentieth century was just beginning.

This was the world in which Elsie was raised. It was the only Newport she knew, and the one she loved. Given that, she was still drawn to the other Newport—the one where Ida Lewis lived and worked. The one outside in the harbor.

It seemed just a matter of course that Elsie Vanderbilt, given her attraction to Lime Rock and fascination with this homegrown heroine, would venture out to the island to meet Ida. After their initial meeting, she was often rowed out to the island, and spent time talking and visiting, while Ida continued her chores.

Even with their obvious age difference of forty years—Elsie was a teenager visiting the now-middle-aged heroine—Ida appreciated the company. Summertime was often chock full of curiosity seekers and visitors, though the stream had somewhat abated over time. She looked forward to her youthful visitor who, with all the graciousness of well-heeled society, still spoke to her with the eagerness and interest of youth. They became friends.

Elsie was twenty years old when she married Vanderbilt in

1901. Their wedding was an opulant affair in typical Vanderbilt style. The ornate wedding cake was in the shape of a trol-
ley, and within every slice was a keepsake piece of jewelry for
each guest. A baby son soon followed, and Elsie spent more
and more time away from her beloved island raising William
Henry III. But when she did come back to visit, she made a
point to spend time with her unlikely friend.

Ida's life had been brushed by the rich and famous, the
legendary and the popular, countless times before. This, however, was the first time in all of her years of being a public figure that she enjoyed the consistency of an actual friendship
with someone whose life was so very different from her own.
Elsie would prove to be a good friend, even after her divorce
from Alfred in 1908. She and her son moved to Tuxedo, New
York, while Alfred made his new home the Plaza Hotel. (Four
years after Ida's death, Alfred would make a trip abroad on the
ill-fated ship *Lusitania,* being one of the 1,201 people to
drown in the sinking of that ship by a German submarine tor-
pedo. Elsie eventually remarried and lived a full, active life in
politics until her death in 1948 at the age of sixty-seven.)

While the Gilded Age in Newport mushroomed, Ida lived
quite a different life, oblivious of the changes. Like many
lighthouse keepers, she spent much of her time tending to her
duties and maintaining the small home. She planted
flowerbeds and kept pets, her favorites being cocker spaniels
and cats. She was also burdened with nursing her ailing
mother, who suffered from stiff joints and chronic pain, and
Hattie, whose lung problems had developed into tuberculosis.
Her youngest brother Hosey had also developed tuberculosis
on the mainland, and was being nursed by his wife of five
years. Her brother Rudolph was unmarried and still lived on
Lime Rock, helping out as assistant keeper and spending some
time at sea as a part-time captain.

Ida still made the papers periodically, especially when she

participated in a rescue or assisted another mariner. Several accounts appeared in the *Newport Daily News* detailing rescue attempts in which she participated but was aided by quicker, faster boats. And Newport Harbor was changing. More pleasure craft and yachts filled a bay that once used to moor only fishing vessels and rowboats. Yachting was becoming the sport of the wealthy, and the Gilded Age was in full swing. More and more people knew how to handle boats, and Ida was now one of many who could capably swing oars.

And she was getting older. Ida was forty-one when Hosey died on June 12 of 1883. The death was expected, but untimely; it was followed later that year by the loss of Hattie, who also died of tuberculosis (the medical books of the time described the disease as "the wasting away of the body due to consumption.") The disease had taken its toll on both siblings, leaving them gaunt and death-like in appearance. The deaths, especially Hattie's, exacted their own toll on Ida, who missed her sister and constant companion dearly. She once commented that she often felt her dead sister with her when she was out on her boat, Hattie's presence making the rowing much easier for her

Her mother took to her bed following Hattie's demise. She had developed cancer and remained an invalid for the remainder of her life. As it was, she had not left the island during the five years that Hattie was critically sick, only tending the light as much as her own illness would permit.

Hattie was the beauty of the family. She never married, most likely because of her illness. A friend wrote to the local newspaper the day after her death, recapping the closeness of Ida's relationship with her. "The two sisters were closely united in their affections and tastes. Hattie possessed rare beauty before her sickness, and was characterized by great amiability and equanimity. Retiring in disposition, the graces of her character were exhaled like the aroma of flowers on sea-girt rocks. Though long possessed of reverent frame of mind, during her last sickness she obtained great peace in the profession of her faith in Christ, and her final dissolution was marked with peace and dignity."

Her sister's own religious devotion coupled with her passing may have led Ida to her next decision.

It was in the year to follow that Ida turned solidly toward religion. On June 8, 1884, she rowed to shore, walked into the Thames Street Methodist Episcopal Church, and was baptized. While having been a member of the temperance movement since her twenties and a follower of Christian dogma, the forty-two-year-old Ida had an underlying desire to make all things concerning her life official. She began to attend church daily, often spending the entire Sunday on shore if her brother Rudolph was home to tend to the light. At night, she and her mother would read the Bible together.

Before Zoradia's death, an article in the *New York Sunday Times* in the late 1880s spoke of the quiet life that Ida had settled into with her mother. The two rarely had visitors save in the summer, but "they are happy—happy in each other's love and daily read the well-worn family Bible and talk of those who have preceded them in the spirit land and with whom they expect to commune in the future."*

When Zoradia died of cancer on July 16, 1887, it was a quiet death. She never awoke from her sleep, and Ida found her seventy-two-year-old mother in bed. She closed the door and quietly rowed to shore. Another chapter of her life had closed.

Ida was now alone.

✦ ✦ ✦

While Rudolph was with her during the latter part of her life (although never appointed a first assistant), Ida never relin-

---

* *New York Times,* Oct. 27, 1911.

Ida with her brother Rudolph on the deck of the lighthouse.

quished full control of the light. "The light is my child," said Ida, "and I know when it needs me, even if I sleep."

Her room was located directly across from the tiny room that housed the lantern, which hung in the room and overlooked the ocean. Even in her sleep, she would sense when the wick needed trimming or when the light had dimmed, and make her way across the hallway and take the large step into the cramped 4- by 4-foot quarters that housed the heavy lamp. Shelves lined the sides of the room, and were stocked with brushes, cutting utensils, polishes, and oil. She would deftly clean the lantern glass and check the oil supply, making adjustments and lighting the beacon for the evening.

"There's a peace on this rock that you don't find on shore. There are hundreds of boats going in and out of this harbor. It's part of my happiness to know they are depending on me to guide them safely." So said Ida.

For most of the last two decades of her life, Ida had won herself a comfortable place in history. She was considered by the press to be the "pet" of the government. In one brief, it

Ida, with Lime Rock Lighthouse in the background, in the late 1800s.

was reported she was receiving special treatment by not having
to conform to the new Lighthouse Service rules, which man-
dated that all in its employ wear the new lighthouse keepers'
uniforms. While it was a regulation uniform expected to be
worn by all, the truth of the matter was that no woman in the
employ of the Lighthouse Service was expected to wear the
double-breasted, blue wool coat with yellow buttons, dark
blue trousers, and cap bearing a metal lighthouse badge.

But while the newspapers may have inflated her status, it
wasn't lost on those on the Lighthouse Board that she had
admirers and protectors who adored her. She was already
being paid more than any of her colleagues in the area.
Records show that Gustave Clark, keeper of Rose Island
Light, was making $500 a year, Charles Schoenemann at
Newport Harbor Light, $600, and Frank Parmell at Castle
Hill Light, $560.

Ida was being paid $750.

The nature of the relationships between keepers was
generally friendly, however, and it is doubtful that her peers

begrudged the aging Ida her salary, especially given her celebrity status and hard-earned reputation.

By 1896, President Grover Cleveland made some changes benefiting lighthouse keepers. He classified them as civil servants, which gave them protections they never had, including the chance for pensions and job stability. The practice of being kicked out of a lighthouse because of a new favored appointee was over, giving keepers a well-deserved sense of permanency.

Ida herself told of other rescues during the latter part of the nineteenth century and early twentieth century. She spoke of saving two men and two children, who cried out for her by name as they clung to an overturned boat. "Ida, Ida Lewis, come save us," they called, which she readily did. She often enlisted the help of Rud on her adventures. Together she and her brother spied a capsized vessel, which happened to belong to a local man, also named Lewis. They fished him out of the marshy area of the harbor, where he was knee-deep in mud, and utterly exhausted. After he revived himself in their kitchen, he told them that after sailing all around the earth, he thought he was going to end up drowning in an old bog within sight of his home.

Ida had many such stories about the rescues that never made it past her lips or the lips of the rescued. But Ida's efforts hardly went unnoticed, especially in the latter years of her life. In 1906, two female friends were rowing out to see Ida. As she waited patiently for their arrival, one of the women stood to adjust her skirts, and toppled into the water. She couldn't swim, and her companion had no wherewithal to pull her in. A sixty-three-year-old Ida dropped her lifeboat from its hanger, and rowed across the water to complete her final documented rescue. (She is unofficially attributed to at least one more rescue three years later, when a group of five girls capsized their skiff, and called for help. She was sixty-six.)

While 1906 proved to a banner year for Ida, it would be one of the last before her star began to fall. Whether she realized it or not, she had a bevy of support behind her, and could count some powerful people as friends. One of them was Admiral George Dewey. Dewey had been appointed Admiral of the Navy in 1899, following an illustrious career in that branch of service, a hero of the Spanish-American War. Ida had originally met him when he was first appointed president of the Lighthouse Board in the 1880s. He often came to visit her, and was fond of their casual conversations. Being from Vermont, he took a strong liking to the Yankee character of the small, courageous woman. She named her cocker spaniel Dewey, in honor of their bond. Ida was also friends with Mrs. French E. Chadwick, who was the wife of Rear Admiral Chadwick, the man who had helped secure her appointment and bestowed the gold medal upon her.

Chadwick was well connected. His wife fretted that Ida's lack of a husband left her with no one to care for her when the inevitable time came that she would have to retire or be retired. A pension would help her immensely. At the time, philanthropist Andrew Carnegie had founded the Carnegie Hero Trust Fund, which recognized the efforts of those who put themselves in perilous situations to save others. In some cases, the Fund gave compensation to those who risked their lives for others, and also awarded a medal in honor of their deeds. Mrs. Chadwick wrote to Carnegie, who thought long and hard about Ida. Unfortunately, he could not add her name to the list. The criteria he developed for his own fund was not retroactive, and all of Ida's perilous rescues happened long before its founding in 1904.

Instead, the altruistic philanthropist gave her money out of his own pocket, in the form of a personal pension of $30 a month. Ida deposited the checks into a savings account for her brother Rud. It was given to him upon her death. And when that unfortunate event occurred, Mrs. Chadwick published a letter that Carnegie wrote to her in response to the news that Ida had passed.

A rare photo of Ida smiling.

"Your kind note gives me one source of satisfaction. A happy and favoured man am I to be enabled to help such heroines as Ida Lewis who has passed away. She had no future to fear, having made the best of this life. Fortunate she was in having you as a friend. Let us try to emulate her in the service of our fellows."

Without any politicking or manipulating, Ida had garnered the support and respect from men such as Carnegie, whom she never met. The year continued to bring good news to the aging keeper.

It was in that same year of 1906 that the American Cross of Honor was incorporated by Act of Congress. The mission of this service was to select one person each year who rendered the most heroic service in saving lives. In a letter dated October 17, 1907, Ida was notified that she was the person they chose. She was the first American woman to receive the honor, which made her a member of the society and garnered her a gold medal complete with certificate. She had been chosen over a multitude of men who had risked their own lives in natural disasters, floods, and large-scale accidents. It was a high honor to be the recipient.

This award also dubbed her the bravest woman in the United States. Ida was riding high. While her life had settled into one of a retired celebrity, she enjoyed spending her days as a devout Christian, continuing to care for the island, her brother, and of course, her beloved light.

✦ ✦ ✦

Ida was not destined to live out her days basking in the glory of her past. Her life took a turn for the worse. Changes were in the wind. Along with the rapid-fire societal changes of the industrial revolution came a new way of looking at things. Bureaucracy flourished. Systems were put in place under the guise of efficiency. What once was simple had now become complicated. Government became laden with layers of red tape, and new, younger superiors were ushered in. Formality and distance took the place of the familiar and well-known. And it infiltrated the Lighthouse Bureau.

Perhaps because of her age and the length of time she actually tended the light, Ida didn't take well to the changes. Supplies had to be accounted for, and under the new systems, forms were required, oftentimes in triplicate. Having to copy something three times must not have made much sense to Ida, who tried her best to comply with the changes. But she made mistakes. And she was curtly reprimanded.

> *Enclosed herewith your Return of Expenditures of oil, wicks and chimneys. You have made an error in subtracting the amount expended for the quarter from the total amount on hand. Correct the same, and return to this office without delay. In the future you will exercise more care in making out this return, as errors made by you delay this office in making its quarterly report to the Lighthouse Board.*

To the woman who had been exalted as both the Grace Darling of America and the darling of the American people, the letter cut deeply. Its impersonal nature was stinging by itself; the additional reprimand left a permanent mark. Ida began to worry. For the first time in her life, she questioned her own performance.

The injustice of the missive was appalling. Privately, she searched for the reason behind it. After all, hadn't she been effectively responsible for the light for almost fifty years? There had never been a complaint, not one negative report under her watch. While other lighthouses had been cited for their lack of order, and even their uncleanliness (which was considered of high priority to the inspectors), Ida had not only kept impeccable vigilance over the lantern—never once missing even an hour during nightfall—she also kept a spotless house. The multitude of reporters to the island often made note of her meticulousness. No, there was never a reason for her performance to come under such scrutiny, such criticism. She began to brood and suffer from nervous depression. She had problems sleeping and took to worrying about her aptitude.

Further problems began to surface when she continued to revert to her usual handwritten notes, requesting supplies and other items, instead of using the appropriate forms. By 1909, the new personnel in the Lighthouse Bureau were beginning to lose patience with what they perceived to be an old lady resisting change.

The reply to your communication of the 27th (February 1909) making requests for 1 barrel of lime, 6 gallons of white paint and 2 gallons of turpentine. You are informed that requisitions for extra supplies at your station should be made on the form provided for that purpose, a copy of which is enclosed.

This type of correspondence continued on and off for the next two years, with each letter digging deeper and deeper into Ida's sense of self-worth, undermining her confidence, and ultimately affecting her health.

By the time she granted a last interview for a full-scale feature piece in *Putnam's Magazine* in 1910, she spoke openly of her health.

"Rud asked me to help him lift a ladder, and he said, 'You haven't got any more strength than a cat.' I told him I was lifting all I could. But lately, I haven't been feeling well—nervous you know. Maybe it's my heart. I don't know. But then, I'm getting old." The title of the article? *A Half-Forgotten Hero.*

Ida had long been one of the Newport attractions. But as she grew older, she grew less tolerant of what was nothing short of rude behavior that was exhibited toward her. In a local newspaper account of September 11, 1909, she exhibited a particular prickliness about her age: "I suppose I am over-sensitive about the age matter, because we all like to remain young as long as we can. But when they tell visitors that I am ninety-eight or one hundred, it is unjust as well as unkind."

Her sensitivity to her age, compounded with criticism from her superiors, only served to make her more susceptible to depression. Feelings of being obsolete and a failure in life soon set in, and things were not about to get better.

In 1910, George Putnam was appointed Commissioner of the Lighthouse Board and made sweeping changes in his administration. Lighthouse keepers in general were older like Ida, who was nearing seventy years of age. Putnam set in motion a plan to consolidate lighthouses by grouping them together and having them maintained by one keeper. He also had them automated. Under the new administration, which was meant to bring the system into the twentieth century, and to improve efficiency through new regulations, many of the lighthouse keepers had trouble keeping pace. In addition, women were allowed to remain as lighthouse keepers only if they could prove that they could do it solo, without the help of anyone else. Ida was fast becoming outdated.

The next year, on September 29, 1911, Ida received another reprimand from the newly appointed commander of the U.S. Navy, who obviously had little knowledge of Ida Lewis or her notoriety. After completing the lengthy ten-page form known as the Annual Property Return, which accounts for everything in the lighthouse right down to a matchstick, Ida received it promptly back in the mail.

> *Your annual property return is herein returned for correction as you fail to take up the following articles . . . Unless satisfactory explanation is submitted regarding these discrepancies, **the fact will be entered on your record.***

Adding insult to injury, Nathan Young, the commander who sent her the missive, didn't even extend the courtesy of signing his name. Its threatening tone implied that Ida had been sloppy in her accounting of supplies and had squandered them.

Its effect was devastating.

Ida was not used to insults and the treatment from the Lighthouse Bureau was tantamount to just that. For the second and last time, Ida found herself slapped in the face by the master she willingly chose to serve for decades: the federal government.

Chapter 9
In Death, Beloved

This is home to me and I hope the good Lord will take me away when I have to leave it.

—Ida Lewis

It was the expedition that would test the very steel of a human being, if indeed any man dare challenge it and come back alive. To early twentieth-century society, it was viewed as the final frontier—the only land mass that had yet to be set foot upon, much less explored. The South Pole was known only as a huge patch of icy tundra, barren and cruel. Antarctica would prove to be the ultimate survival contest, as it pitted two explorers against each other in a race against time.

The distance to the South Pole and back was 1,766 miles and every step of it was done on foot, in temperatures that never rose above 0 degrees Fahrenheit. The journey was a constant battle with record snowfalls, blinding blizzards, food deprivation, and frostbite. Knowing all of this, Roald Amundsen (1872–1928), a Norwegian polar explorer, launched his expedition to the South Pole on October 20, 1911. He set out with four men, sleds, and a massive team of dogs. Ten days later, British explorer Robert F. Scott would embark on his own expedition to the South Pole.*

And more than halfway around the world, just one day after Amundsen began his journey, faint streaks of orange and pink were crisscrossing the horizon of the Atlantic Ocean. Dawn was breaking on the small island of Lime Rock, as another hero made her way across the hallway to the tiny lantern room just steps from her bedroom. She deftly opened the beveled glass of the sturdy Fresnel lens. She carefully wiped the black carbon that had built up overnight, and checked its clarity. She would later return to the light to make sure that the oil was filled and the lantern readied for its next overnight vigil.

The sum total of Ida's life was encompassed in that flame. "The light is my child, and I know when it needs me, even if I sleep," she said.

---

* Amundsen did reach Antarctica on December 14, 1911, winning the race to the South Pole. His team spent three days at the pole and then left a Norwegian flag and letters to both the king of Norway and Robert F. Scott before returning.

Perhaps Ida would have better identified with Robert F. Scott, the stalwart British explorer who lost the race to the South Pole, but paid the ultimate price in doing so. Scott and his expedition reached the South Pole on January 16, 1912, to find to his dismay, the tent and flag of his competitor, who had arrived well over a month earlier. Their return journey met with disastrous weather and the entire party perished. Their frozen bodies, along with valuable documents and specimens in their tent, were found eight months later.

One of Scott's last diary entries reveals his valiant spirit: "Had we lived I should have had a tale to tell of the hardihood, endurance, and courage of my companions which would have stirred the heart of every English man. These rough notes and our dead bodies must tell the tale."

It was the child she never had, the center of her small
world. It divided her days into a touchable, tangible routine,
giving her life a steady continuum.

It was a duty from which she drew most, if not all, of her
identity. "There are hundreds of boats going in and out of
this harbor," she once said. "It's part of my happiness to know
they are depending on me to guide them safely."

The flame dictated her life. It ruled her time, but she
drew great comfort in knowing that it gave her life purpose.
Even though the world hailed her for saving the lives of
eighteen people, there was a greater motivation for Ida. It
was out there beyond the faintest rays of her light. It was the
collage of all those she saved because she kept the light and
provided them with a beacon of safety: the faceless mariners,
the nameless ships, the unknown schooners. It was for them
that she kept the light. It was for the countless numbers she
would never know, those she would never row out to rescue
in the face of gale winds, those for whom she would never
risk her own life, those who would never taste a hot molasses
toddy. It was for those who were doing their job well, just as
she was doing hers.

She was their mistress, with the sole charge of keeping
them out of harm's way. It was those unnumbered sailors
who were saved every night by the mere existence of the light
itself. And it was she, Ida Lewis, who had the weighty mission
to keep it burning. There must have been thousands upon
thousands whom the light saved with her faithful assistance.
So many the world would never know about because their
names would not be etched in newsprint, or uttered on the
lips of society matrons, or recounted by children searching
for a hero to worship.

She extinguished the flame on October 21, 1911, for what
would be her last time.

Ida crossed the hallway and dressed for the day. She made

her way downstairs to bring in a bundle of wood from outside to stoke the fire in the kitchen and to make breakfast for her brother Rud. Carrying the armload of wood, Ida collapsed to the floor. Wood tumbled around her. She suffered a massive stroke, commonly known in the day as apoplexy.

Her brother awoke at 7:30 A.M., surprised and somewhat dismayed that his sister had let him oversleep, wondering her whereabouts. He wandered from room to room calling for her. He found her body on the floor of the kitchen in front of the hearth, logs all about her. He rushed to her and listened to her chest. She was still alive, and after trying to bring her back to consciousness, Rud succeeded in reviving her. Ida asked him to call for their doctor, and slipped back into unconsciousness. She would never speak again. Rud had to leave his sister unattended to row to shore to find the doctor and bring him back to the island, sick at the prospect that she may be dead upon their return.

"She was semi-conscious," he later told the *Newport Daily News.* "I did what I could for her, but as I knew aid had to be summoned. I was forced to leave her alone while I rowed ashore . . . When I returned to the lighthouse, my sister had grown much worse and had lost all consciousness."

The following three days marked a deathwatch in the local newspapers, and the story was picked up by newspapers as far away as Europe. Ida was popular all over again. Though she had receded subtly into the background of society's fickle tapestry of celebrity, she never left its heart as the Grace Darling of America.

Upon hearing of Ida's condition, the War Department sent a missive requesting that Fort Adams artillery practice be suspended in deference to her condition, as those with her sent word that the loud shelling seemed to agitate her.

Hundreds of telegrams arrived from the distinguished to the unknown, wishing her a return to good health. Mrs. Elsie

Vanderbilt, upon reading the news of Ida's stroke, left her home in Tuxedo, New York, early the next day to travel to Harbourview. She was rowed out to the island and spent a few final hours with the unconscious heroine, her friend.

Ida remained in a deep coma until shortly before eight on the morning of Tuesday, October 24, 1911. It was then that Idawalley Zoradia Lewis Wilson slipped into a quiet death at the age of sixty-nine. At her side were her brother Rud, her doctor, and several close family friends, including Mrs. Amelia Shaw Kerr, who would handle all the funeral arrangements and viewing of the body.

There was no question in the minds of those who knew her well—especially her brother, who was quite outspoken to the local press—about why she died so suddenly. Her stroke, they said, was due to stress. That and the nervous depression brought about by ongoing changes in the Lighthouse Department that had led to the formal reprimands Ida had received.

Being chided was not easy for Ida to stomach, especially since she had a meticulous sense of duty, and had likely grown used to being highly valued. She was also a historical figure who had the uncommon vantage point of watching herself become a legend in her own lifetime.

So it was no surprise when exaggerated and inflammatory reports appeared in the local newspapers. The *Newport Daily News* ran a subhead directly under her obituary headline that read, "Fatal Illness Probably Due to Worry over Department Reports."

Adding more fuel to the fire was a rumored report circulating just days before she collapsed. According to the October 19 *Daily News,* new plans were under discussion to reconfigure the buoying and navigational aids in Narragansett Bay. The piece strongly suggested that Lime Rock Light was under scrutiny, with a real possibility of it being abolished altogether and Ida being removed as its keeper. The newspaper also ran a photograph of Ida along with the story, which ended on a somewhat dour yet hopeful note, referring to the gold medal Ida received from Congress years before. "It is suggested that in view of what Congress did in regard to Ida Lewis that body may take a hand if it is proposed to abolish her lighthouse."

In fact, on the day before her death, the newspaper sent a telegram to the Lighthouse inspector, with the single line: "Is Lime Rock Light to be abandoned?" The response? "No information to that effect at this time."

Upon reading the story, or at least hearing of its rumored content, Ida, who had already been deeply questioning her competency and suffering great consternation over the Lighthouse inspector's curt treatment, had fallen into dark despair. In light of the rumored decommission, her words were eerily prophetic. She once said, "This is home to me and I hope the good Lord will take me away when I have to leave it."

Her wish was granted. That day, the steamship *Priscilla* from the Fall River Line plaintively tolled its bell as it steamed past Lime Rock, in honor and tribute to its former mistress.

The sea was inordinately mild, or as the *News* recounted, "as calm as a millpond and the last water voyage was made under the most pleasant conditions." Ida's body made its last trip across the familiar route from Lime Rock to Wellington Avenue in downtown Newport on the morning of October 27. She was accompanied by the undertaker and harbormaster on that final trip.

Her brother Rud stood stoically on the rocks of their island home and watched as the body of his dead sister left the island for the last time. "That is the way poor Ida wanted to leave the light when she left for good, in her casket."

A large number of people gathered on the shore as her body was removed from the transport boat and taken to Thames Street Episcopal Methodist Church, where she laid in state from 10:00 A.M. to 2:00 P.M. The casket was open,

draped with a silver broadcloth decorated with column cor-
ners and surrounded by an abundance of large floral arrangements. A single arrangement given by the Sorosis Society of
New York was placed on the closed end of the casket, and a
simple silver plate bore the inscription:

Ida Lewis
Died October 24, 1911
Aged 69 years

Throngs of people streamed by her coffin to take a last
view of this contemporary heroine. One report estimated
some 1,439 visitors paid their respects. *The News-Newport*
reported:
"They saw a peaceful face, a little thinner perhaps than
many remembered, but without any suffering. The hands,
thin and showing her age and work more than the calm features, were crossed over her breast. They were the hands of
one who had worked, strong hands which seemed able to do
the task they were called upon to perform with the oars and
which had proved this for so many long years and under so
many varying conditions."
Dignitaries flocked to the service as well, the government
being represented by Admiral R.P. Rodgers and Rear Admiral
Chadwick. Other mourners included fellow keepers, mariners,
a flock of men from the lifesaving station located in Newport,
as well as a number of prominent wealthy Newporters, cottagers, and local residents.
Appropriately, Fort Adams played a prominent role in the
funeral proceedings. The pallbearers were six soldiers from the
encampment, and the Fort Adams band played select hymns
during the service, as well as afterward during the processional
to the gravesite.
The Reverend Stanley C. Hughes, rector of Trinity, spoke

of the dead heroine as being "the most remarkable woman Newport ever produced."

Then Reverend W.F. Geisler, pastor of the church, rose from his seat and captivated the public with his stirring eulogy.

"Let no one think that Ida Lewis can be buried," he said. "Her worn-out form may be placed beneath the clods, but still will there come the traveler from near or from far to look upon her grave . . . . To him, will she still be alive and so will be with us. We will tell our children, and our children will tell their children the tale of the rescues of this lighthouse keeper in the harbor of Newport. She achieved immortality.

"The life of this unique woman is its own best eulogy. She herself opened the door and was welcomed into that high society—the aristocracy of heroism, the great of heart. To her the need was the duty, the cost was never counted. There were no terrors to her of wind or wave or rock or freezing cold. The cry of distress alone struck fear and courage and action into being and when even the light did not avail to warm and guide, she went down into the waters, among its perils, to the rescue, as if it were an ordinary task."

He continued to extol her courageous heart.

"This was not, however the work of flesh and blood, of nerve and muscle alone. The strength and steadiness of muscle and nerve—a strength and steadiness born of simple temperate life—were indeed requisite to her. Heroic efforts and yet they would have been soft untwisted flax without a great spirit and a will of steel. To this spirit the heart of this wonderful woman, we bow today and do honor unto ourselves. As the light that she so faithful was a beacon to the mariner with the circle of its reach, so the light of her brave unselfish spirit became an inspiration of courage to the whole world, the fame of her deeds having filled it. She who seldom went beyond the limits of her native city, became a citizen of the world—her name, a household treasure because she kept the light shining and feared not the duty perilous."

The spillover from the attendance in the packed church filled the street outside, at least seventy-five yards in either direction. Carriages lined the streets and a large number of cottagers were in attendance. Mourners lined the route from the church to the cemetery, where the body was interred following an elaborate funeral procession, which included two carriages overflowing with floral arrangements and six soldiers solemnly carrying the casket.

The gravestone of Ida Z. Lewis, located in the old cemetery off Farewell Street in Newport, R.I.

In honor of her passing, stores in the business district shut down, and flags were voluntarily and ceremoniously kept at half-staff on public buildings such as the customs office, public schools, and city hall, and on most of the ships in the harbor. The bells in the harbor rang in unison to honor her passing.

Ida's body was committed to the ground that afternoon, placed in a burial site next to the graves of her father, mother, and sister in what was called Old Cemetery, or the Common-ground on Farewell Street in Newport. Her epitaph read: *The Grace Darling of America, Keeper of Lime Rock Lighthouse, Newport Harbor.*

So ended the life of Ida Lewis. It was not necessarily a happy one and never could be characterized as carefree. She spent most of it caring for others, performing mundane, backbreaking tasks, and watching over the light at Lime Rock. But it was a life she herself chose. If anything, she fought to retain her simple world in spite of her early notoriety. While she remained unchanged and untainted by the attention society gave her, there must have been part of her that identified with the "Heroine of Lime Rock." Above her bed hung a framed picture of Grace Darling's gravesite. Perhaps in some corner of her heart, she did view herself as the American Grace Darling. Maybe it inspired her to live up to the expectation the world had placed before her. She never did want fame, and she never reaped much from it. And she never once ventured a foot on the path to which it could have led.

Chapter 10
Epilogue:
Ida Lewis Lighthouse

Our good deeds, although registered in heaven, are by our fellow sinners but too often buried with our bones.
—Colonel George Brewerton, Ida Lewis biographer

The light of Lime Rock passed out of the hands of the Lewis family for the first and last time several weeks after Ida's death. Her brother Rud took over as interim lighthouse keeper on the day of her demise. He had sent a correspondence to the Inspector of the 3rd District the day before she actually died. Knowing the end was near for his dear sister, Rud informed the man that he was prepared to continue tending to the light, because of his sister's condition.

Now unconscious due to a severe stroke of apoplexy . . . her condition is critical. I have accordingly taken

charge here since then, since I have lived with her in
cooperation for nearly 25 years. Until the course of
conditions change, one way or the other, I presume I
am expected to continue in this capacity.

The telegram was barely sent, when he had to send
another, notifying the Bureau of his sister's death. He received
a telegram in reply from the Inspector.

Your telegram has just been received. This office
desires to express sympathy and regret for the death of
your sister, Mrs. Ida Lewis Wilson, former keeper. If
you will continue to care for the light until a new
keeper can be sent to relieve you, your kindness will be
appreciated.

Even if asked to take over the position, Rud was so dis-
traught over Ida's passing that he found being alone on the
island unbearable. He left the island two weeks later. Evard
Jansen was appointed for $516 a year (compared to the $750
Ida had been making at the time of her death). Jansen had
been a lighthouse keeper at Sandy Hook in New Jersey, following a lifetime of service in both the Army and Navy. He
remained on Lime Rock until it was deactivated in 1927. He
and his wife had a baby daughter while on the island, whom
they named Ida Lewis Jansen.

Rudolph, having no family members save three half-nieces
who were born to his half-brother Joseph in Massachusetts,
moved off Lime Rock after living there most of his life. He
moved in with family friends, Mr. and Mrs. Edgar Kerr, in
the seaport area of downtown Newport. He died of a cerebral
hemorrhage at Newport Hospital on November 9, 1917,
almost six years to the day that he left Lime Rock.

Ida did not leave a will, but had made it known that she

wanted all of her valuables and memorabilia left to the Newport Historical Society. Her personal belongings were shared in common with her brother Rudolph for most of the latter part of her life, and he inherited them. The pension so kindly transmitted to her from Andrew Carnegie was transferred to her brother.

Barely two months had passed after Ida's death, when the movement was launched to change the name of Lime Rock Lighthouse to Ida Lewis Lighthouse. It appears the desires of local Newporters fell on deaf ears at the Bureau of Lighthouses.

Shortly after Ida's death, on November 15, 1911, Horatio Wood of Newport sent off a letter to his U.S. Senator, George Peabody Wetmore, who was out of the country at the time. Wood was a member of the Cadets of Temperance and a staunch supporter of Ida Lewis. When Wetmore returned a month later, he sent a copy of the letter along with his own note to George Putnam, the Commissioner of the Bureau of Lighthouses. The response came within five days, stating that "lighthouses and other aids to navigation are without exception named according to their geographical position, and any departure from this system or change in the name of an aid when not essential, would in the opinion of the Bureau be undesirable, as liable to be confusing or dangerous to mariners."

It is not known whether Ida's fears about the rumored decommissioning were grounded in truth. In his correspondence to Senator Wetmore, Commissioner Putnam made reference to the discontinuance, the rumors of which had obviously reached him (even larger newspapers with wide circulation reprinted the theory that Ida's stroke was brought on by concerns about the lighthouse and her own performance).

"I beg to state that it is not contemplated, so far as the Bureau is informed, that this light shall be discontinued, and its discontinuance has not been considered," Putnam stated.

That said, he still went on to deny even bringing the proposal to change the name of Lime Rock Light before the Bureau for the safety navigational concerns stated above.

The letter from Putnam seemed to suffice for Senator Wetmore and presumably Mr. Wood and the others backing the idea. The issue of renaming Lime Rock in honor of Ida Lewis seemed to have been by and large forgotten.

More than a decade later, the correspondences resumed between members of the General Assembly from Rhode Island and the Bureau of Lighthouses. And this time, the result would be dramatically different.

The first letter appears in early 1923, written by Representative Clark Burdick, congressman for the 1st District in Rhode Island, asking the Bureau to investigate reasons why the lighthouse could not have its name changed. Unlike his counterpart in the Senate of more than a decade earlier, Burdick took on the mission with a plan. The point man for a local movement in Newport, where varying groups were circulating a petition amongst Newporters, the gentry, and working class, Burdick had tremendous grassroots support. And he didn't take "no" for an answer.

What's not clear is what prompted the movement to be resurrected, or why it should crop up so many years after Ida's death. Perhaps it was because the townspeople and Rhode Islanders in general had taken to calling Lime Rock the Ida Lewis Light. "Lime Rock" had been completely abandoned as its name. Whatever the reasoning, Burdick took up the torch for the swelling throng of Newporters who had circulated a petition to have the name formally changed.

In a brief letter in response to Burdick's request for information, which the Bureau hoped would close the matter once and for all, the acting commissioner once again cited "regulations for governing the Lighthouse Service do not permit complying with your request." But Burdick was persistent, asking for the specifics of the so-called regulations and waited patiently for a month while the Bureau of Lighthouses stalled. Finally a letter arrived in May, in which Putnam made little effort to veil his elation. "I take pleasure in quoting you the following extract from the 'Regulations of Lighthouse Service 1918.'"

He quoted: "The name recommended for an aid shall, when practicable, include the name of the locality to be marked, and in that case should be taken from the most recent charts of the United States Coast and Geodetic Survey . . ."

Burdick knew now that his initial correspondence with the Bureau of Lighthouses was as futile as Wetmore's earlier request. The same administration was in place and he received the same reply about navigational safety being tied to the geographic naming of each lighthouse. Acknowledging receipt of Commissioner Putnam's letter, Burdick said he understood that the Bureau could not take favorable action on the name change because of the cited regulations. He didn't let it stop with the niceties:

"In your first letter, it was spoken of as a universal rule, and I presumed that perhaps it was unwritten law, or precedent, which can be broken. An instance of this is when Ida Lewis was appointed a keeper, when no woman had ever before so appointed, as I understand it."

Then he cleverly asked that Putnam send him a copy of the regulations so he could "turn it over to my friends who advocated the change."

Whether or not Putnam did this is unknown. What is known is that Burdick decided to go to the source: the U.S. Coast and Geodetic Survey, which was responsible for the nuts-and-bolts surveying of properties and had been cited by Putnam as the deciding body for the names of lighthouses. His thinking was acute. In December of 1923, Burdick sent off a letter outlining his proposal for the name change. "I presume that your Bureau, with the authority vested it in for compiling charts, can recommend a change in name in such an instance as this."

If the survey could come up with no good reasons for not renaming the island, and he could get them to agree with his position, it would add more political pressure to the Bureau of Lighthouses and specifically, Commissioner Putnam, to reverse the decision.

During this time, more and more organizations including the Sons of Temperance, private citizens, mariners, and the like added their names to the growing petition, adding momentum to what was becoming a full-scale movement across the state of Rhode Island.

What may have been fueling Putnam's opposition to the name change was hinted at in a letter from the First Assistant Superintendant, the lighthouse inspector for the district in which Lime Rock was stationed. In correspondence to the commissioner, he urged that any change might interfere with the decisions that were already being made regarding Lime Rock. The lighthouse "is of practically no use, and it is the intention of this office, as soon as funds will permit, to do away with the present light structure, and establish in its place an unwatched acetylene light." If the name was changed to Ida Lewis Lighthouse, the concern was that people would be up in arms over its discontinuance.

It was all a moot point, for in less than a month, the Coast and Geodetic Survey came back with its reply. The officials fully and enthusiastically endorsed the idea. At its monthly meeting in February, it approved the name change with the provision that the Lighthouse Bureau agreed. A letter was sent to Putnam, encouraging his Bureau's endorsement.

In conjunction with the approval of the government agency, the Rhode Island General Assembly passed a resolution favoring the change, as did the City of Newport. At the time, the *Providence Journal* came out with a lengthy article about the movement to change the lighthouse name, detailing the life story of Rhode Island's heroine, and drawing further public support for the movement.

Defeated, Putnam gave in, and the Bureau gave its approval of the name change, being the first and only time such an honor was paid to a lighthouse keeper.

Automatic lights were fast replacing the lanterns of a bygone lighthouse era. The new acetylene lights did not have to be maintained like the old ones, and given the new lighthouse on Goat Island and other navigational aids, the Ida Lewis Lighthouse was beyond practical function as a navigational aid to mariners.

The lighthouse was deactivated in 1927, three years after its renaming.

Jansen and his wife and child left the island house when the new tower with the automated light was erected. It fell into disrepair. Townspeople watched as the paint began to chip away from the brick edifice. The shuttered windows broke open from the whipping wind from the sea, and the doors banged. What once was the neatly kept home of their beloved heroine was falling apart.

Oddly, while all of her belongings of worth and medals had been bequeathed to the Newport Historical Society, much of it still remained in the home. It was later collected by the members of the Ida Lewis Yacht Club, who turned it over in the 1950s or 1960s, according to membership, to the Newport Historical Society.*

Dr. Horace Beck, a leading Newporter, couldn't bear to see that happen. According to his wife, who recalled the series of events that saved the lighthouse many years later, it was a

---

* Sadly, the Newport Historical Society only has several items of Ida Lewis memorabilia. The staff claims to have received only the items in its possession. Her medals, the silk pennant from Jim Fisk, and other items are missing at press time.

joint decision between Beck and philanthropist Arthur Curtiss James to buy the lighthouse from the government. As only a small part of the island was actually being used by the government (for the skeleton tower for the automated light), it was readily agreed to. Mrs. Beck recalled the action:

> *When Ida Lewis Light was decommissioned, it was put up for sale in New York. Dr. Beck heard of it the day before it was to be auctioned off and it was said that the fishermen were going to buy it for a place to sort their catch, the discard of course to be thrown overboard. When Dr. Beck came home for dinner that evening, he remarked what a splendid yacht club it would make. In talking it over, I suggested he get in touch with Mr. Arthur Curtiss James. He telephoned Mr. James who concurred with the yacht club and said to get down there and buy it, and how much to pay. Time was short but we reached Newport Long Wharf just in time as the New York boat's gangplank was being pulled in. The captain was an old friend, saw him and had the gangplank put back. At the auction, Dr. Beck realized that the fishermen were determined to have the place and that the price would be in excess of what Mr. James had mentioned. Luckily, Mr. James was reached by telephone and his succinct answer was, "You want to buy it, don't you?"*

In 1928, the newly formed Narragansett Bay Regatta Association bought the lighthouse and most of the island for $7,200, to preserve its history and create a perfect site in desirable Bretton Cove for a yacht club. Later that year, the Ida Lewis Yacht Club was officially organized, and was listed among Newport's clubs for the first time in 1929. Ceremoniously, on the Fourth of July, 1929, a full sixty years to the day that Newport celebrated Ida Lewis Day, the Ida Lewis Yacht Club opened its doors. Its flag is a small lighthouse encircled by eighteen stars, one for each of her rescues. (The official total varies from eighteen to twenty-five, depending on sources.) The first commodore was, appropriately, Arthur Curtiss James, and his beautiful yacht Aloha became the honorary flagship. Charter members of the Ida Lewis Yacht Club included descendants of the Newport elite, including the Astors and Vanderbilts.

A wooden walkway was built to the rock by James, and the house was renovated and turned into a clubhouse. Floats and ramps were added. The house was kept as it was for the most part, with no structural changes. The club keeps what was the kitchen decorated with Ida memorabilia, and the grounds have the same pristine feel they must have had when Ida lived there and tended her gardens on the shiny white island. Housed in the old light tower is a replica light, the real lantern currently on display at the Newport Historical Society Museum. The club currently has 375 members, many of whom moor their boats in Bretton Cove.

At the opening ceremony, Commodore James spoke of his feeling for the future of the club, as his large yacht was the lone vessel sitting in the harbor. "My chief ambition for this yacht club is the revival of small boating. As a boy I lived in Newport. There were hundreds of small sailing vessels and frequent races were held. This interest in boating diminished as I grew up. I am anxious to bring back those days."*

His wish has been granted. Newport is synonymous with boating, and on a clear summer day, as far as the eye can see, the horizon around the Ida Lewis Yacht Club is dotted with seafaring vessels.

Ida Lewis is also remembered by the U.S. Sailing Associa-

* *The Evening News,* July 5, 1929.

The trophy for the Ida Lewis Regatta.

tion, which is the governing body for the sport of sailing. They have regatta classification for women, and the annual Ida Lewis Regatta is a women's two-person junior event. Held on the lake in Oklahoma City, Oklahoma, it is a great sailing venue with its ever-present blowing winds, fresh, clean water, and lack of motorboats and jet skis. While Ida never sailed, she rowed, and the spirit of the competition honors her tremendous accomplishments.

In 1963, the Coast Guard, which had taken over the Lighthouse Service in 1939, deactivated the light altogether. The yacht club later received special permission to put a light back in the old lantern casing; it is still lit today as a private aid to navigation.

In special honor to lighthouse keepers, the U.S. Coast Guard came out with a new class of boats: the Keeper Class coastal buoy tender. Honoring those who tended America's lighthouses, the cutters are named after keepers. The first vessel of this class was christened *IDA LEWIS*. The *IDA LEWIS* is docked in Newport and is a state-of-the-art, 175-foot vessel that takes daily and overnight trips around coastal Rhode Island to check positions of buoys and maintain them. The U.S. Coast Guard also dedicated a training center to Ida Lewis in Cape May, New Jersey, in 2001.

The men of the cutter were granted permission by the city council to refurbish Ida Lewis' gravestone, which had fallen into a state of disrepair. The new monument will include a display of 4-foot granite pillars shaped like lighthouses. A steel chain will connect the pillars.

The U.S. Coast Guard continues to honor the past while continuing the tradition of seeing mariners safely through the night and storm.

It is a mission that is carried out in the spirit of Ida Lewis.

Notes

There are several myths about Ida Lewis that needed to be clarified in the writing of this book.

Carnegie Hero Trust Fund: In particular conflict with many accounts of her life is the persistent belief that Ida Lewis was a recipient of the Carnegie Hero Trust Fund, now the Carnegie Hero Commission based in Pittsburgh, Pa. One curious mistake has been the continual belief that Ida was an awardee of the trust. According to the Commission's historian, there is no record of Ida Lewis Wilson ever being an awardee of a medal or of a pension, as has been reported in other accounts. The fund was started in 1904 by Andrew Carnegie and honors those who risk their lives in saving others.

But what I did find and included in this text was newspaper documentation verifying that since Carnegie could not go back on the rules of his own commission and give her the honor retroactively, he could do it himself, independent of the commission. It appears that he compensated Ida monthly out of his own pocket, to ensure she was taken care of in her old age.

Marriage: According to quoted accounts of her brother Rudolph, Ida and her husband lived together for two years before she returned home. Other sources point to the connubial marriage actually lasting only several months. Since Ida had not officially been appointed, there is no way to verify the length of time she was away. There are no letters or notes exchanged between her family and her during the period she was away that have survived to the present day.

Opinions differ as to whether Ida Lewis and her husband first took up residence in Newport or Connecticut. Since an overwhelming number of accounts state that they were married for several years (and taking several to mean two), that would have them married from Oct. 23, 1870, to at least late 1872. Although an exhaustive search through Bridgeport city records and newspaper accounts unearthed very little regarding this matter, an entry for "William H. Wilson" listed as a "seaman" owning a house in Black Rock appears out of the blue in the Bridgeport City Directory for the year spanning 1872–1873. If the names were collected during the year prior to printing, that would mean he was living there in late 1871. This places him within the time frame of his connubial marriage to Ida, whose name would not necessarily appear next to his as she was not the owner of the house. It is deduction but I believe a reasonable one.

Death: According to most newspaper accounts, Ida Lewis died of apoplexy, or stroke, which occurred on the morning of Oct. 12, 1911. She lingered and finally passed away three days later. However, *Notable American Women (1607–1950)* accounts for her death differently, saying she died from a cerebral hemorrhage. Her vital statistics concur that it was a stroke that killed her.

There is also some discrepancy in the dates, according to different tertiary sources, regarding the deaths of family members. Death and marriage records found at Newport City Hall were used in this book as the source of these dates and relative information.

Rescues: There is confusion about the second rescue. According to Brewerton, there were three soldiers in the skiff, and two jumped overboard. Other accounts, including *Putnam's Magazine,* place the number at two, with one of them being a soldier, the other being a young boy who he had hired to row him home. This could be a confusion between two rescues, or just simply wrong. Since Ida herself sanctioned the writing of the Brewerton booklet and other accounts concur, his account of the incident was the one adapted.

Appointment: It has been passed down through several generations that Ida Lewis was the first female appointed a lighthouse keeper. A lot would depend on the definition of an appointment. This changed over time, as one given from the President to one that the Secretary of the Treasury granted. As far as I could discern, other women were appointed as keepers, perhaps not with the formal letter and hefty annual pension that Ida received, but appointed nonetheless. Prolonged research into this issue would clear up the matter.

Bibliography

While many were investigated, not all possible sources have been used. The following books, newspaper articles, and reports have been utilized in compiling this book.

Achincloss, Louis. *The Vanderbilt Era: Profiles of a Gilded Age.* New York: Charles Scribner's Sons, 1989.

Adamson, Hans Christian. *Keepers of the Lights.* New York: Greenberg, 1955.

Annual Report of the Commissioner of Lighthouses to the Secretary of Commerce and Labor for the Fiscal Year Ended June 1911. Washington: U.S. Government Printing Office, 1911.

Annual Report of the Light-House Board to the Treasury for the Year 1868. Washington: U.S. Government Printing Office, 1868.

Annual Report of the Secretary of the Treasury on the State of the Finances for the Fiscal Year Ended June 30, 1939. Washington: U.S. Government Printing Office, 1939.

Bachand, Robert. *Northeast Lights: Lighthouses and Lightships (Rhode Island to Cape May, NJ).* Norwalk, Conn.: Sea Sports Publications, 1989.

Basler, Roy P., ed. *The Collected Works of Abraham Lincoln.* Abraham Lincoln online.org.

Bassett, John Spencer. *A Short History of the United States.* New York: The Macmillan Co., 1927.

Beard, Charles A. and Mary R. Beard. *The Rise of American Civilization.* New York: The Macmillan Co., 1939.

Brewerton, Colonel George A. *Ida Lewis, the Heroine of Lime Rock.* 1869.

Carruth, Gorton and Associates. *American Facts & Dates.* New York: Thomas Y. Crowell Company, 1956.

Cherry-Garrard, Apsley G.B. *The Worst Journey in the World; Antarctic, 1910–1913.* New York: Lincoln MacVeagh/The Dial Press, 1930.

Clifford, Mary Louise and J. Candace Clifford. *Women Who Kept the Light: An Illustrated History of Female Lighthouse Keepers.* Williamsburg, Va.: Cypress Communications, 1993.

Conway, John S. *The United States Lighthouse Service 1923.* Washington: U.S. Government Printing Office, 1923.

Curti, Merle. *The Growth of American Thought.* New York: Harper and Brothers, 1943.

Encyclopedia Americana. New York and Chicago: Americana Company, 1948.

The Evening News, July 5, 1929.

Frank Leslie's Illustrated Newspaper, August 1869.

The Growth of the American Republic (1865–1942). New York: Oxford University Press, 1942.

"A Half-forgotten Heroine," by J.E. Clauson, *Putnam's Magazine,* February 1910.

Hamm, William A. *The American People.* D. C. Heath and Co., 1939.

Harper's New Monthly Magazine, April 15, 1869.

Harper's Weekly, July 31, 1869.

Hicks, John D. *The American Nation.* New York: Houghton Mifflin Co., 1941.

Hockett, Homer C. *Political and Social History of the United States (1492–1828).* New York: The Macmillan Co., 1925.

Holland, Francis Ross, Jr. *America's Lighthouses: Their Illustrated History Since 1716.* Brattleboro, Vt.: The Stephen Greene Press, 1972.

James, Edward T., ed. *Notable American Women. A Biographical Dictionary, Vol. II (letters) G–O (1607–1950).* Cambridge, Mass.: The Belknap Press of Harvard University Press, 1971.

Johnson, Arnold Burges. *The Modern Light-House Service.* Washington: U.S. Government Printing Office, 1890.

The Journal of the U.S. Life-Saving Service Heritage Association, no. 12, Fall 1999.

Keeper's Log, Fall 1986.

"The Life Saving Benevolent Association of New York and its Medals," Captain Jack Boddington. *The Journals of the Orders and Medals Research Society,* vol. 24, no.3, Autumn 1985.

MacDowell, Dorothy Kelley. *Commodore Vanderbilt and his Family: A Biographical Account of the Descendants of Cornelius and Sophia Johnson Vanderbilt.* New York: D.K. MacDowell, 1989.

Marcus, Jon and Susan Cole Kelly. *Lighthouses of New England.* Stilwater, Minn.: Voyageur Press, 2001.

McCullough, David. *The Great Bridge.* New York: Simon and Schuster, 1972.

Mitford, Jessica. *Grace Had an English Heart.* New York: E.P. Dutton, 1989.

Morison, Samuel Eliot and Henry Steele Commager. *The Growth of the American Republic (1000–1865).* New York: Oxford University Press, 1942.

Muzzey, David. *The United States of America—From the Civil War.* Ginn and Co, 1924.

Nettels, Curtis Putnam. *Roots of American Civilization.* Crofts, 1938.

Nevins, Allan. *A Brief History of the United States.* New York: Oxford University Press, 1942.

— *Ordeal of the Union,* New York: Charles Scribner's Sons, 1947.

— and Henry Steele Commager. *A Short History of the United States.* New York: Random House, 1943.

The New International Year Book, 1946. New York and London: Funk and Wagnalls Co., 1946.

New York Herald Tribune, April 16, 1869.

New York Times, Oct. 25, 1911.

— Oct. 27, 1911.

New York World, Oct. 31, 1932.

Newport Daily News, various clips from Aug. 5, 1869–Oct. 29, 1969.

Newport Herald, October 28, 1911, various clips from July 5, 1869–Oct. 16, 1911.

Newport History: The Bulletin of the Newport Historical Society, vol. 61, 62, no. 209–216.

Oceans, (published by Oceanic Society), November 1985.

Patterson, Jerry E. *The Vanderbilts.* New York: Harry N. Abrams, Inc., 1989.

The Providence Sunday Journal, Feb. 17, 1924.

Putnam, George R. *Lighthouses and Lightships of the United States.* Boston: Houghton Mifflin Company, 1933.

A Record of Newport Deaths, vol. 5, 82, 194.

— vol. 7, 120.

A Record of Newport Marriages, vol. 1, 129.

Revolution, July 15, 1869, 26.

— Sept. 2, 1869, 129–130.

Schlesinger, Arthur Meier. *Political and Social Growth of the United States, 1852–1933.* New York: The Macmillan Co., 1939.

Smith, Darrell Hevenor and Fred Wilbur Powell. *The Coast Guard: Its History, Activities, and Organization.* Washington: The Brookings Institution, 1929.

Snow, Edward Rowe. *Famous Lighthouses of America.* New York: Dodd, Mead & Company, 1955.

— *Famous Lighthouses of New England.* The Yankee Publishing Company, 1945.

Twenty-Fourth Annual Report of the Commerce 1936. Washington: U.S. Government Printing Office, 1936.

U.S. Coast Guard. *Historically Famous Lighthouses.*
Washington: Public Information Division, U.S. Coast
Guard, 1972.
Weiss, George. *The Service: Its History, Activities, and
Organization.* Baltimore, Md.: The Johns Hopkins
Press, 1926.
Wright, Louis B. *The Atlantic Frontier.* New York: Alfred A.
Knopf, 1947.

Photo Credits